THE LIBRARY OF HOLOCAUST TESTIMONIES

A Cat Called Adolf

The Library of Holocaust Testimonies

My Lost World by Sara Rosen
From Dachau to Dunkirk by Fred Pelican
Breathe Deeply, My Son by Henry Wermuth
My Private War by Jacob Gerstenfeld-Maltiel
A Cat Called Adolf by Trude Levi
An End to Childhood by Miriam Akavia
A Child Alone by Martha Blend
The Children Accuse by Maria Hochberg-Marianska and Noe Gruss
I Light a Candle by Gena Turgel
My Heart in a Suitcase by Anne L. Fox
Memoirs from Occupied Warsaw, 1942-1945
by Helena Szereszewska
Have You Seen My Little Sister?
by Janina Fischler-Martinho
Surviving the Nazis, Exile and Siberia by Edith Sekules
Out of the Ghetto by Jack Klajman with Ed Klajman
From Thessaloniki to Auschwitz and Back
by Erika Myriam Kounio Amariglio
Translated by Theresa Sundt
I Was No. 20832 at Auschwitz by Eva Tichauer
Translated by Colette Lévy and Nicki Rensten
My Child is Back! by Ursula Pawel
Wartime Experiences in Lithuania by Rivka Lozansky Bogomolnaya
Translated by Miriam Beckerman
Who Are You, Mr Grymek? by Natan Gross
Translated by William Brand
A Life Sentence of Memories by Issy Hahn, Foreword by Theo Richmond
An Englishman in Auschwitz by Leon Greenman
For Love of Life by Leah Iglinsky-Goodman
No Place to Run: The Story of David Gilbert by Tim Shortridge and
Michael D. Frounfelter
A Little House on Mount Carmel by Alexandre Blumstein
From Germany to England Via the Kindertransports by Peter Prager
By a Twist of History: The Three Lives of a Polish Jew by Mietek Sieradzki
The Jews of Poznań by Zbigniew Pakula
Lessons in Fear by Henryk Vogler
To Live is to Forgive ... But Not Forget by Maja Abramowitch

Frontispiece: Vienna, 1927, Grandmother Ullmann's sixtieth birthday. The author, aged three and a half, is on her grandmother's left. Her father is on the extreme right of the back row, with her brother Pierre standing in front and her mother seated on the extreme right.

A Cat Called Adolf

TRUDE LEVI

VALLENTINE MITCHELL
LONDON • PORTLAND, OR

First published in 1995 in Great Britain by
VALLENTINE MITCHELL
Crown House, 47 Chase Side
London N14 5BP

and in the United States of America by
VALLENTINE MITCHELL
c/o ISBS, 5824 N. E. Hassalo Street
Portland, Oregon 97213-3644

Website: www.vmbooks.com

British Library Cataloguing in Publication Data

Levi, Trude
    Cat Called Adolf. — (Library of Holocaust testimonies)
    I. Title   II. Series
    940.5318

ISBN 0-85303-289-0

Library of Congress Cataloging-in-Publication Data

Levi, Trude.
    A cat called Adolf / Trude Levi.
        p. cm. (The Library of Holocaust testimonies)
    ISBN 0-85303-289-0
    1. Levi, Trude. 2.2 Jews – Hungary – Biography. 3. Holocaust
survivors – Biography. 4. Holocaust, Jewish (1939–1945) –
Personal narratives. 5. Hungary – Biography. I. Title. II. Series.
DS135.H93L4855 1994
940.53'092–dc21   99-18872
[B]   CIP

Typeset by Regent Typesetting, London
Printed in Great Britain by MPG Books Ltd, Bodmin, Cornwall

Contents

List of Illustrations

Frontispiece: Vienna, 1927, Grandmother Ullmann's sixtieth birthday. The author, aged three and a half, is on her grandmother's left. Her father is on the extreme right of the back row, with her brother Pierre standing in front and her mother seated on the extreme right.

The Library of Holocaust Testimonies

It is greatly to the credit of Frank Cass that this series of survivors' testimonies is being published in Britain. The need for such a series has long been apparent here, where many survivors made their homes.

Since the end of the war in 1945 the terrible events of the Nazi destruction of European Jewry have cast a pall over our time. Six million Jews were murdered within a short period; the few survivors have had to carry in their memories whatever remains of the knowledge of Jewish life in more than a dozen countries, in several thousand towns, in tens of thousands of villages, and in innumerable families. The precious gift of recollection has been the sole memorial for millions of people whose lives were suddenly and brutally cut off.

For many years, individual survivors have published their testimonies. But many more have been reluctant to do so, often because they could not believe that they would find a publisher for their efforts.

In my own work over the past two decades, I have been approached by many survivors who had set down their memories in writing, but who did not know how to have them published. I realized what a considerable emotional strain the writing down of such hellish memories had been. I also realized, as I read many dozens of such accounts, how important each account was, in its own way, in recounting aspects of the story that had not been told before, and adding to our understanding of the wide range of human suffering, struggle and aspiration.

With so many people and so many places involved, including many hundreds of camps, it was inevitable that the historians and students of the Holocaust should find it difficult at times to grasp the scale and range of the events. The publication of memoirs is therefore an indispensable part of the extension of knowledge, and of public awareness of the crimes that had been committed against a whole people.

Martin Gilbert
Merton College
Oxford

Introduction

One day, in 1949, just after I had arrived in Israel I sat in the waiting room of the Sochnut (the office for administration of new immigrants) awaiting my turn to go into the office. There were a number of others with me. In Israel people talk. They ask questions. Someone asked me where I came from. I said: 'From South Africa'. Then someone else asked: 'Are you South African?' I do not remember in what language the conversation took place: English, German, French, maybe a little bit of Yiddish mixed in, or was there someone who spoke Hungarian? It could not have been in Hebrew for I did not as yet speak the language. One question followed another and then someone said: 'You know, you do not have to answer every question.' I was taken aback, for I did appreciate that in that short space of time I had told half my life story to these people I had never seen before and have never seen since.

And yet I often answered questions and told stories about my life. People used to say: 'Why do you not write it down? It would make a good book.' Or: 'This is a story films are made of!'

Well, now I have written it down. I had lots of encouragement, first from my husband who steam-rollered me into using a word-processor. He also supported me, criticised me and reminded me of incidents I had forgotten to mention.

Stella Hyams spent hours reading through the manuscript and correcting my English – I am infinitely grateful to her. Pauline Paucker did a large number of corrections. Professor Joe Baylen worked through the manuscript with a fine tooth comb while recovering from a heart attack and, finally, Judith Schecter presented me with two pages of very worthwhile corrections.

1

Lionel Simmonds worked through the manuscript with love and care. I am most grateful to all of them. I also had much encouragement from many who read the manuscript. They all said: 'It must be published; do not give up hope.' And last but not least, I very much value all the sympathetic effort put in by the staff of the publishers, and would like to thank them and especially Mrs Norma Marson, who edited the book with great care.

One question I have been asked again and again over all these years: how did I manage to keep sane through it all? I have no clear answer and am still puzzling this out. Keeping a sense of proportion, a sense of humour, a lack of envy and trying to see the good side of things, yet still remaining realistic: facing up to events as they came and not feeling too sorry for oneself: I am not sure if all these add up to an answer, but it is possible. Judge for yourselves.

Trude Levi
London, 1994

1 • *Looking back in anger*

Forty years, I thought, would have made all the difference. Up till then I had always resisted invitations to go to Germany. However, as we were going to be nearby and would have a car, it was an opportunity to spend a few days with some old friends.

Everyone we met was friendly, kind and helpful. Frau Emmy, too. She must have been about 70. She kept the little village shop and looked after her garden and cats. We bought a few things from her; and she gave us herbs and salad from the garden without accepting any money. We talked about her garden, we talked about her cats. She had a dozen of them, small cats, big cats. And then: 'This one is a funny one – it always raises its paw – we call it Adolf.'

It was as if someone had hit me on the head. I suddenly realised what had been wrong with me throughout the holiday. This was what I had feared. I could not wait to get out of Germany as fast as possible. It was the people of my age and older; the fear that I might have to shake hands with someone who had taken part in the killing of my parents, my friends ...

I suppose I was just lucky to survive and am now able to tell the tale. But that cat really upset me ...

It is most important to speak out, to tell it all, not only what happened to me in the Nazi concentration and work camps, but my life before and after that grim experience. For many have spoken about the horrors of the camps, but few have discussed the effect they had on those who survived the ordeal. Most people assume that once you have survived, all is well and life goes on as usual. And, if there remains a trauma, it will fade in time. But how one's everyday life was affected by the experience few people realise or understand.

I was young – only 20 at the time – and in spite of having had a

major operation, I must still have been very strong. Hungary was
not occupied by the Nazis until March 1944 and this left only a year
or so for the Germans to deal with the Hungarian Jews. But a year
can be very long in such circumstances. I was herded into a ghetto
in May of that year, imprisoned in a local concentration camp seven
weeks later and deported to Auschwitz on 7 July 1944. The following month I was transferred to a Buchenwald outcamp, Hessisch-
Lichtenau.

My behaviour in camp was not very prudent because I seemed to
lack a sense of survival. I did nothing to be ashamed of. I suppose
my attitude did help me to survive, not only physically but also
morally. The very fact that the Germans could not crush me or
reduce me to a subhuman being or destroy my self-respect was a
personal victory. It was a strong sense of self-respect which kept me
going. I tried and, I believe, succeeded in remaining a decent
human being throughout. And being non-religious – an agnostic – I
had to believe in myself.

In the concentration camp I felt, and I believe I was, an outsider. I
find this difficult to explain. Since I had no sense of survival and no
fear, I behaved in a non-rational way. If you wanted to survive, you
had to be selfish and not care what others felt; to try to possess
things, even to snoop – anything to be in the good graces of the *Kapo*
(camp leader) or the SS women. To work as little as possible to save
one's energies, to steal if there was occasion and not to share – all
these were things I did not do. And I despised all those who did. I
shunned the company of those who compromised, and I was
certainly not very lovable. Yet it was my way of surviving, even
though I did not really care whether I survived or not. Not that I
wanted to die. I just was not willing to do anything that would have
lowered my self-imposed strict moral standards which were so very
important to me at the time. This attitude, I firmly believe, enabled
me to survive against all odds.

Looking back I now think that inwardly I was very much a loner.
This may be the reason that I remember so little about my camp-
mates. I was not very tolerant either of what at the time I considered
as weaknesses.

Also I must have been somewhat smug. I was not vain as a young
girl and did not think that I was good-looking. I did not believe in

4

make-up and hairdressers. My view was that one must be natural in every way. One should be liked for what one is, not what one tries to show of oneself. A decent person has nothing to hide, speaks the truth and looks as she was created. Hence I did not accept make-up, and I did not understand the motivation of the women in the camps who tried to hide their shaven heads with kerchiefs, or who altered the rag-dress we were given. I always looked like a scarecrow; my dress was too long and I was certainly not going to shorten it – at least it kept me warm when it was cold. I rather despised those who spent time on beautifying themselves. At the time I did not understand that one dresses to please oneself.

Recently I read a survivor's memoirs in which she was often preoccupied with fear of being used as a prostitute for the German Army. It did not even occur to me that the SS might wish to sleep with any of us – I was too naive to imagine such a thing. On the other hand, I am sure it would have made me keep myself looking even more unattractive, for I certainly would not have agreed to sleep with any of them and would have probably been shot or gassed if it had come to it. Luckily this problem did not arise.

At the Buchenwald outcamp of Hessisch-Lichtenau, we were confined to our barracks at certain times, and since we were not often given water to wash ourselves, in wintertime, during the night, I would slip out and wash in the snow, even though I risked being shot on the spot. As a young girl I was not terribly keen on washing; a bath or shower, yes, but washing bit-by-bit with cold water was not my favourite way of keeping my body clean. Yet in the camp, it became an obsession to keep clean. I just had to wash myself and felt that my survival depended on it.

We were about 32 to a room in the barrack in Hessisch-Lichtenau. Our bunks were in two rows on both sides of the room – upper and lower bunks. In my room there were a number of women from my home-town, whom I had known most of my life. But somehow I had very little contact with them. Many I do not even remember. One of the reasons was that we worked in three shifts and thus I hardly saw some of my mates. They were either at work or asleep when I was free and awake. As I was always a night owl I had difficulties with the early morning-shift but none with the night-shift which most others found unbearable, so every third week I

5

tried to find someone who was ready to swap. It was dark when we went to work. In the factory I usually worked alone and not in the group and thus had little contact with my mates.

I do remember the two Günsberger sisters, Ella and Olga. They were gentle unmarried women who ran a beauty-parlour in my home-town. Their niece, Jutka Rothschild, from a town called Sümeg, had lost her mother early. She used to spend her holidays in Szombathely and though she was younger than I we became friends – as we still are. Ella and Olga got themselves into the favour of the SS women, who used to come into our barrack to have hair-dos and facials and be made up. I refused to speak to the two women for I thought that they had sold themselves.

There were also the two Kohn sisters, who had had a wool-shop in Szombathely. They were older, rather colourless. They did some sewing for the SS women. Again I did not want to have any contact with them. One girl, a couple of years my senior, and her mother were extremely aloof and seemed to be more friendly to the *Kapo* Manci than to anybody else. They seemed to imply that they were superior to others. I was most upset about their behaviour for, at one time, before I went to study in Budapest, I had been friendly with the daughter and had become very fond of her. But somehow this seemed to have been forgotten by her, and I remember the feeling of being treated by them rather like a stranger. I could have been wrong, but that was the way I felt at the time.

Then there was Magda Szemző, who had been my French and art teacher at school. She used to be my favourite teacher and I still think that she was the best teacher I have ever come across. Though Jewish-born, she had been baptised as a child and was a very religious Catholic. I used to idolise her. Now I felt extremely disappointed in her. She used to spend most of her free time on her knees praying to 'Our father . . .'. She influenced Gerti Polgár, also an ex-student of hers, into her religious practices. She took to it like a duck to water and prayed with her. They were in bunks opposite me. I was unable to understand at the time that this was their way of coping with our fate. As I was anyway extremely anti-religious and certainly had no respect for the so-called Christians who treated us in such an inhuman fashion, I just could not understand how they dared to pray a Christian prayer.

6

There were two mothers with twelve-year-old daughters: Mrs Dénes, wife of a lawyer and mother of the charming Gabi, and the spoiled Mrs Weisz, wife of an architect and mother of Mitzi. These two girls had convinced the SS at the selection that they were 16 and thus managed to remain with their mothers. At the very first selection when we arrived all the children under 16 and adults over 40 were separated and either killed straightaway or used for experiments and killed subsequently or in the process. They were not considered strong enough for hard labour. But these two managed to get through and were both in our room. When I occasionally volunteered for extra work and received an extra soup I usually gave it to Gabi whom I liked a lot. She was everyone's favourite.

Puci Dukesz was the one to whom I felt closest in the whole room. She came from my home-town and though I had known her all my life somehow I had never spoken to her before. She was the wife of a jeweller or antique dealer in the same house in which we had lived. For some unknown reason she was considered an outcast: a girl from a poor background marrying a rich man, and was never accepted into so-called good society. I never found out why. She had a nephew who lived in Budapest and visited them frequently. He was a good-looking fellow, a rich, charming, playboy-type, and was very much in love with me. I quite liked to be with him and was rather flattered, but when he asked me to marry him I said no. This was the last time I saw him before he was sent to the front with a Jewish forced-labour company as a guinea-pig on the minefields, where he perished. Poor Ákos Strauss. Puci was always fair, always undertook any task that was unpleasant but had to be done, and I often joined her. I am sad that in all these years I have been unable to get in touch with her. I would love to have seen her again.

In the room I can remember only two other women. Neither was from my home-town. I did not like them. One was a much older person, actually in her sixties, who had somehow managed to keep out of the selection. Later she was the one who betrayed me to the Germans when I denied that I knew German, which actually was my mother-tongue. Her betrayal nearly cost me my life (see pages 16–17).

The other woman was a thief. She stole from me anything that I possessed, which was practically nothing. But twice I was given a cloth to put into my wooden clogs and during the night she stole it. She also stole from me any bread I had saved to eat later, or pieces of paper which I managed to lay my hands on and bound with string into a sort of book. I hated her. I felt that it was beneath my dignity to fight with her and she quite openly flaunted whatever she had taken. I was too naive and could neither understand nor forgive that someone could steal from a fellow inmate.

I was very fond of two girls, twins, from Bratislava, Éva and Hedva Weisz. Éva was short with glasses and Hedva was tall and slim. I was also very fond of a Transylvanian girl, Grete Wurzel, an attractive blonde who spoke Italian.

There were others whose names I do not remember. When we had time to spare, we recited poems which I then recorded in my 'book', and we sang together. They often asked me to sing and I loved to do so. With Luciana, our Italian camp-doctor, I struck up a friendship which has lasted to this day.

Working on the night-shift, I seldom had time to talk to anyone. Except during *Zaehl-Appell* (roll-call) I slept during the day. Roll-calls could be harsh. We were lined up in rows of five, first thing in the morning and again in the afternoon. We stood for at least half an hour, but sometimes for several hours, as a torture or punishment. In the factory, except for the first week or so, I worked on my own and had little occasion to speak to people.

In the munitions factory, where during the first few days I worked on the conveyor belt, we worked with German women. The foreman ordered us to sing. On the second day I began to sing the 'Lorelei' and the Germans all joined in. I was pleased because I knew that the song was banned in Germany, the words being by Heine, the music by Mendelssohn, both of whom were of Jewish origin. The foreman angrily ordered us to stop singing the song. We obeyed, but I had achieved a moment's triumph.

After the war, as a consequence of what happened to me, it was not possible to resume normal life. The fact that the Hungarians had treated Jews badly motivated my decision not to return to Hungary. As a result I lost my Hungarian nationality and became a stateless person. I quickly discovered that to be stateless was also to be an outcast, unwelcome to live or work, even if grudgingly allowed to take up temporary residence. Decent people today are horrified at condoning or participating in the horrors of the Nazi era, but I sometimes wonder if they do not protest too much!

A few years ago there was a film called *Mephisto*,[1] which I consider to be more important than most other films about Nazi Germany, illustrating as it does significantly what can happen to pervert someone who fundamentally has the best intentions. It tells the story of a liberal German actor, who has Jewish friends, and has a coloured girl-friend. Initially, he is violently opposed to the Nazis, but as time goes on one can see how slowly, though inexorably, through fear and ambition, he is manipulated into exactly those situations he has previously criticised. He begins by betraying his friends and denouncing people, without perceiving what is happening to him. Ultimately he has become a completely different person.

I understand his predicament and as a result find myself in some difficulty. I want to explain to people what happened yet I sometimes feel it would be pointless. How does one prevent people from being manipulated?

Fear is a very strong and powerful emotion and, unfortunately, also a very strong motivator. Therefore, to some extent I can understand what happened to people in Germany. I do not think that everyone was culpable. I think that very many people did nothing. They did not get involved or want to get involved even if they witnessed events of which they did not approve. They did not speak out because there are very few heroes. Heroes sacrifice family and livelihood or at least take the risk of sacrificing all that they have achieved. Therefore I do accept excuses.

Years later, when I was working at the Wiener Library, London – the main library in Britain dealing with the Holocaust – many German researchers came to make use of the collection. Some would say that during the Second World War they knew nothing about the Holocaust. Similarly, when I lived in South Africa, some Germans I encountered there also pleaded ignorance of the machinations of the Third Reich. This excuse I absolutely refused to accept. But when some Germans admitted: 'Yes, we did know what was going on, but we were too frightened of losing our jobs or being

9

deported or being arrested and questioned if we had dared to speak out' – that I could accept.

I am often appalled at injustice inflicted on people in Britain and elsewhere and although I express resentment I rarely if ever do anything about it. It was not always so. When I was young, before my trust and faith in humanity had been destroyed, I too demonstrated and believed and even took considerable risks. I deeply resent having had to relinquish my cherished faith and beliefs, but now, because of my experience, I accept this as a normal, if not very attractive, human trait.

I was one of a group of a thousand Hungarian women who were transferred from Auschwitz to a Buchenwald outcamp to work in a munitions factory. We were marched through villages to reach the factory and there we worked with Germans. Our heads were shaven and many of us walked barefoot in the snow. We marched in rows of five and were dressed in clothes that did not fit. On our backs an enormous number was sewn for all to see. There were hundreds of groups like ours in Nazi Germany working in factories as slave-labour. There were also many soldiers in Poland either working in the camps or near the camp of Auschwitz, as well as the railwaymen who transported us, who knew what was being done. Although we were emaciated, we were not invisible. And so if someone says to me: 'We did not know', I know that they are prevaricating. But if they say: 'We knew, but did not do anything about it', I would accept that as an explanation of what occurred.

When we came out of the ordeal alive – as I did – what were my feelings? My emotions were varied. One was the realisation that human beings are capable of doing everything and anything to their fellow creatures. It took me a very long time indeed to come to terms with that. Perhaps it took even longer to comprehend the behaviour of my fellow inmates. Today, I can accept it more readily because I understand that it was their means of survival. Nevertheless, there were incidents which then I found difficult to comprehend. One incident still confuses me – although by now I am able to find an explanation for it.

When we were working at the munitions factory we were suddenly told that we were to be paid three Deutschmarks per day. We received the pay for each of the following three days. On the fourth day a shop was opened and we were told to spend our money there. The choice was limited. For nine marks one could buy either a piece of writing paper, an envelope and a stamp, or a lipstick. We could borrow a pencil and send a letter to members of our family in Auschwitz from whom we were separated – by that time most of them had been exterminated in the gas-chambers or, if very lucky, had been transferred to some other work-camp. Whatever, it was a cruel joke, relieving us of those nine marks. Even so, several women wrote letters since they could not believe their relatives were no longer alive.

The other option was the lipstick, and that is what baffled me. These women – my co-inmates – who were starving, had no clothing apart from what they had on their backs and were in a dreadful emaciated state, fought for those lipsticks. There were not enough of them to go round and here they were kicking and pummelling each other in order to possess one stick or even one of the right colour. It made me feel sick to see them fighting over such trivia. Today I try to convince myself that they acted as they did to preserve what was left of their femininity. I must be lacking something, but I still cannot accept such behaviour, especially since it provided the German guards with a good deal of amusement.

The men in the camps seem to have organised themselves much better. From accounts written by Primo Levi[2] and other survivors, they managed to obtain things which they could barter. Maybe we also had things available but was I too naive to notice?

I had two possessions. As my feet were large and the boots issued were too small for me, I sometimes received clogs – although most of the time I was barefoot. I have already told how the cloth I was twice given to put into my clogs was stolen from me both times, though I was the only person in my room who needed it. My other possession was the odd leaves of paper (printed on one side) which I had managed to 'organise' (steal), and the small piece of string with which I bound the leaves into a 'book'. I had no compunction about stealing these items, but appreciated the danger involved. This book was my most cherished possession until I lost it during the Death March which I shall describe later. I certainly had nothing to exchange or trade. Primo Levi wrote that if you had no spoon, you had to lap up your food. In Auschwitz-Birkenau, we certainly

11

had no spoon and we had to lap up our food. For meals we stood five in a row with the shrewdest in the first and the silliest (me) mostly in the fifth row. The so-called soup came in one big pot and people swigged from it and passed it on. By the time it reached the fifth row, there was usually hardly anything left in the pot. Here was a prime example of the survival of the fittest!

I suppose that at Hessisch-Lichtenau we did have a spoon, though I do not seem to recall it. There came a time when food was so scarce that a spoon would have been of no use anyway.

At Auschwitz, Birkenau B Lager, everything seemed greyish-yellow to me. Not a blade of grass between the barracks. When we were inside one of the barracks there was no space even to lie down. There were 1,200 women to each barrack. The only way all could be accommodated was by sitting in rows back to back with knees pulled up, feet touching. That was how we slept during the four weeks we were at Birkenau. If you had to go to the latrine – and most of us suffered from dysentery, rumours being spread that some drug had been added to our food – we had to climb over bodies to get to the exit. Some women began to scream and then the guards would shoot into the barrack. Once you had got out, to get in again, to secure another sitting place in a row, was a very difficult feat indeed.

Twice a day at least we were called out for *Zaehl-Appell*. Early in the morning it was freezing cold; then it became warmer and swelteringly hot and we were forced to stand interminably in rows while the sun blazed down on us. There was no escape, nothing to drink. On arrival we must have been given some other drug (or so it was rumoured) that had caused our menstrual period to begin. We had no underpants, nothing to keep the blood from dripping on to our legs or on to the ground. That was the ultimate degradation and it was the last menstrual period many of us had in camp. The body does not waste reproductive energy on starving humanity in severe shock.

We were not allowed to enter the barracks during the day. We sat in the dirty greyish-yellow dust or wandered around. One day a group of women drew a circle and an alphabet on the ground and held a seance. I did not believe in such things, but had nothing better to do, so I stood by and watched. They had found a piece of glass and moved it around the circle – or allegedly it moved of its own momentum. After all sorts of moves there came a jubilant shout that 'Hitler had been assassinated'. Why was it that I suddenly said with complete conviction: 'Yes, but he did not die'. How did I know? And how did I dare? It was the first time I had a premonition. I felt an absolute compulsion to speak out and was nearly lynched for my pains. But I was right. It was the attempt on Hitler's life of 20 July 1944, which he survived. I could not have known of the event for we had no contact with anyone outside and no news whatsoever.

One day when our bread was being distributed, our *Kapo* gave a smaller piece to a twelve-year-old girl who was there with her mother. I told the *Kapo* to give the child the same as we received. She refused and I became angry and attacked her. *Kapos* were the stand-ins for the SS women. They wielded great power. There was silence. Would she send me to my death? If she denounced me to the authorities that could have been the end for me. But Manci the *Kapo* gave the child an additional piece of bread and from then on she respected me. I never had any more problems with her.

Another day we were called out for *Zaehl-Appell* but this time we first had to strip naked. Usually roll-call was carried out separately for each barrack, but on this occasion we had to go to the main barrack square. Everyone had to be present, we were told, for a medical inspection. We stood there from early morning in the intense cold through the heat of the day, until late at night, when it was freezing again, with no food or drink. Many fainted and once they dropped they were taken away and never heard of again. And then camp commandant Hoess came with the camp doctor, Mengele, and some other SS officers. They passed one by one in front of us and they looked down our throats and at our hands. And there we stood in all our nakedness without even our hair, which, on arrival, had been shaven off our bodies.

One day I heard music, Mozart's 'Eine kleine Nachtmusik'. Was I hallucinating? Here, in this barren wasteland, the strains of Mozart! Women started to run, all in one direction. I followed and the music became louder. On a rostrum there was a small women's orchestra playing. I began to cry – such music in this hell! What torture was this going to bring us? What devilish tricks were they playing on us

13

now? Since I used to play the cello, I spoke a few words to the cellist when the music stopped.

A hand touched me. A tall girl, head shaven – it took me some time to recognise my cousin Marianne. She was the daughter of Uncle Róbert, my father's younger brother. She was brought up in the same village where my grandmother lived, in Zalaszentgrót. When we were small children we used to spend holidays together and were very fond of each other. Marianne was brought up a Christian. Her mother was half-Jewish and her father had converted to Christianity. Her mother died when she was 13 and her father remarried. Since her fourteenth year her parents had enrolled her into a boarding school where no Jews were accepted. It was a most anti-Semitic school and from then on my friendship with Marianne ceased. She had learned to play the piano and was quite gifted. Now she stood near me, holding my hand and crying and begging me not to leave her. We were in different barracks and in the end had to separate. I felt very sorry for her. At least I knew and accepted that I was Jewish and that what had happened to me was because I was Jewish. But after her anti-Semitic and elitist upbringing, to be in an extermination camp must have been incomprehensible for Marianne. In me at least she found someone from her past who had been attached to her. Now we had to be separated. Luckily Marianne survived.

That evening, three-and-a-half weeks after my arrival in Auschwitz-Birkenau there was a selection. Later we were gathered for further processing and during the night, while they began to tattoo us with our camp number, there was an air-raid. The lights went out and the tattooing stopped. I was among those who escaped being tattooed. In the morning, we were loaded into railway cattle-trucks and were transported to the Buchenwald outcamp, Hessisch-Lichtenau, to work in the munitions factory which was some five miles from the camp. For the first three or four days the conditions were marvellous. We were given clean clothes, even underwear, which we did not have until then. There was a bathroom with clean bowls and plugs. Unfortunately, some inmates could not resist taking the soap and the plugs with them and did not keep the bathroom very clean. As a result the camp commandant decided that we were pigs and shut off first the warm water and later the bathroom as well most of the time. The huts in which we were quartered had about twenty two-tiered bunks, with a mattress on each bunk, and had central heating. Unfortunately, the heating was switched on when we arrived in August, the bedbugs came out, and the heat was intense.

The bugs were especially attracted to me; wherever I slept they congregated on my body and tormented me. By the third night they completely covered me and I soon became a most welcome sleeping guest in all the huts. If I was there hardly anyone else was bitten. I seemed to have the sweetest blood of all. Unnecessary to say that the heating was turned off when it got really cold.

Meanwhile, conditions deteriorated as time went on, though in a different way our life in the camp became only moderately better than at Auschwitz. We had a camp commandant about whom I still have ambivalent feelings. He was an SS officer but he was not a sadistic man and did not do things from outright cruelty. He did everything according to the rules. There were two incidents of special importance to me, which I recall under his regime.

We were told that if anyone escaped and was caught she would be executed. One day two girls managed to escape, but they were caught and returned to the camp. We were called out for *Zaehl-Appell*. They brought the two girls and gave them spades with which to dig graves for themselves. When the graves were ready they were shot and we had to bury them there and then. During all this time we stood on *Zaehl-Appell* and we were told that this was an example of what would happen if anybody else attempted to escape.

The commandant made a point of ensuring that we received our bread rations. They were larger in the beginning and got smaller as time went by, but at least we got our piece of bread every day, however small, in equal portions until the day our commandant was summoned to Buchenwald for consultations. Then for the two days of his absence we did not get our bread rations.

I overheard a conversation between two of our SS women guards who spoke in my presence, assuming that I did not understand German. My mother was Viennese, and my first mother-tongue was German, although I grew up in Hungary and was equally fluent in Hungarian. At home we always spoke German, especially when my mother was present, for her Hungarian was not very good and we were not very patient with her. I have always admired English-speaking people for their tolerance of foreign accents and faulty syntax, for most Central Europeans lack such tolerance and forbearance.

But I am digressing. The two guards were saying how pleased they were that they had managed to sell our bread while the commandant was absent. As an afterthought they asked one of my room-mates if I really did not understand German. I had always denied any knowledge of the language during my time in the camp. However, my room-mate told the guards that not only did I understand but it was my mother-tongue!

They were also aware that the commandant knew me. Occasionally he used to call for volunteers. If you volunteered you had the chance of getting an extra bowl of soup. But if no-one came forward and people were forced to undertake the work, they were treated quite badly. I often volunteered with Puci, who was in charge of our room, and we used to give the extra bowl of soup to the two children – both twelve years old – who were with us in the room.

One day the commandant's dog died and he needed volunteers to bury the animal. It was hard work for it was winter and the soil was frozen. Puci and I volunteered for the job. The commandant thanked us for it and henceforth often greeted me.

Now the two SS guards feared that I might inform the commandant of what I had overheard. They came to me and said that they knew I understood German and offered to appoint me as a work-leader. I told them that I did not want the 'promotion' because I did not wish to push other prisoners around. Most other inmates would have been overjoyed to obtain such a privileged position for it meant extra rations and other perquisites. At the time, I was working like a horse, barefoot, often in the snow, pulling a heavy metal trolley loaded with 40 grenades each weighing some 44 lb, down a very steep slope, in constant danger of being crushed against a heavy metal door at the bottom of the incline. It was particularly dangerous because I had to rely on whoever was handling the brake so as to avoid being crushed if I was not quick enough to jump aside as the trolley accelerated downhill. Also, when the trolley jerked, grenades often fell off. I still have the mark on one toe from a grenade which fell on my foot. However, this was a task for which I had volunteered in order to get away from the conveyor belt in the munitions factory. At first I had had the task of tightening the top of the grenades with a spanner, which would have driven me insane had I continued to work on it for a longer period. (It reminded me of Chaplin's film *Modern Times*.[3])

Shortly afterwards the two SS women guards who had earlier approached me took me to the place where we usually assembled for *Zaehl-Appell* and told me to remain there. Slowly, one by one, more inmates came as the rumour spread that it was a sort of selection. The weak were being taken to a paper factory where the work was not so heavy. In one sense I did not care what happened to me for I was feeling completely exhausted. When all those to be selected were lined up, the commandant came with the camp-doctor, Luciana Nissim. They inspected and counted us. It turned out that there were 208 persons when there should have been only 206. I only found out later that Luciana had been directed to supply the numbers of the sick whom she saw every week. That week the number was 206. The Germans were always so meticulous: if 206 were required in a selection there could not be 208.

The commandant and Luciana took me and one other person out of the group. No-one ever heard anything of the other 206 inmates again. There is a record available showing that they were taken back to Auschwitz where presumably they all perished in the gas-chambers. A list has survived the war of the names of the 206 women who were taken away. It is in alphabetical order and in the space where my number (20607) and my name (Mosonyi, Gertrud) should have appeared an obvious correction (01) is visible. The same occurs with another person where (02) has been inserted. The list is still in my possession.

Many times we spoke with Luciana who had some qualms about having helped to save me. She feared that it might be construed that she had helped a personal friend. Of course, her fears were groundless; I had not been on the sick-list and, moreover, it was the prerogative of the commandant as to who would be selected. Many years later, Luciana told me that she was upset how naive I was at the time. (At the time she thought that I had volunteered to go away and did not know that I had been put there by the SS guards.) She knew that the rumour of selection for work at the paper factory was untrue and that those taken were destined for death.

My feelings for the camp commandant (*Sturmscharfuehrer* Wilhelm [Willi] Schaefer) therefore were ambivalent. As I remarked earlier, he was not a sadist. On the other hand, his supervisor, Ernst Zorbach, who came once a month from Buchenwald for two or three days, went out of his way to be vicious. When he was in camp everybody was terrified. The man was a psychopath who revelled in our misery. By contrast, Schaefer, though a weak character, was not a brutal individual. I never felt that he took pleasure in our misery, though he was punctilious in executing every regulation. Was that perhaps why I could not hate him?

Many years later, during the early 1950s, I was spending a few days' holiday at a guest-farm, run by friends in South Africa. One evening there was a fierce tropical storm, with pouring rain and frequent thunder and lightning flashes. It seemed as if the storm would never end. We were in the dining-room in the middle of our meal when a car pulled up in the forecourt of the guest-house. A family entered: a tall man, a woman and three or more children. I glanced at the man at first without any special interest. Then I had a flash of recognition. It was none other than Willi Schaefer, the camp commandant at Hessisch-Lichtenau. I began shaking and my friends looked at me, puzzled. They knew that I had been in a concentration camp in Germany. When I told them who the man was, the owner went up to him, told him that he and his family were not welcome and asked him to leave the dining-room. He would not be sent away – the storm was still raging – but it was arranged for dinner to be served in his room. He and his family were requested to depart early in the morning and to remain in their rooms until then.

Now why did I not expose him to the authorities? Was it because I knew it would not help? I had heard that many Nazis had escaped to South Africa and were accorded not only refuge but a cordial welcome. Or was it because I did not feel that strongly about him? And why did I not confront him and tell him who I was? I certainly do not remember having felt the need to denounce him; I had no desire for revenge. Was I just too shocked? I never saw the man again. When a few years ago I received Dieter Vaupel's[4] book *Das Aussenkommando Hess. Lichtenau des Konzentrationslagers Buchenwald, 1944/45*,[5] I realised that no-one knew where Schaefer was or what had happened to him after the war. He had simply disappeared.

We usually walked the long distance to the factory from the Hessisch-Lichtenau camp. At times we were taken part of the way by train. It must have been for the night-shift on which I often worked. The railway station was unlit and it was a pitch dark winter's night. When the short train – usually two or three wagons – pulled in, one had to scramble on quickly. One day I found myself in a compartment alone, or so I thought. I started quietly to sing the Brahms 'Lullaby'. Suddenly a male voice asked who was singing in German so pleasantly. It was one of our Wehrmacht guards. He came up to me and started a conversation. How was it that I knew German so well? Had I studied music before the war? He seemed a decent enough man functioning in that grim environment. He asked me if I had ever played the recorder. I told him that not only did I play it, but that I was trained to teach it to children in a nursery school. He said he would ask his daughter to send him a recorder for me. When we arrived at our destination he resumed the normal official tone. But from then on, whenever I saw him he repeated that he had written to his daughter and he had a few kind words for me. Once he even got me a bowl of soup – real soup – from the officers' mess, but the recorder never arrived.

In the munitions factory, when pulling the trolley with the grenades, I often worked with a particular German worker. We rarely spoke to each other because to do so was strictly forbidden. But it was sometimes possible to converse as we worked outside in the dark completely on our own. The man gave me to understand that he was secretly a communist and was very distressed at our treatment. He had seven children and life was not easy for him. From time to time he would bring me a sliver of bread or a small onion, always wrapped in newspaper. He would give it to me, saying gruffly that I should go to a certain corner to eat it – the corner was lit – making sure that I could read what was written. I had to return the newspaper to him after having glanced at it. There was always some news in it that cheered me up. Something bad happening to Germany.

19

Previously, I mentioned that I had been working with a trolley on a very steep slope. While this man was about I was not afraid of an accident at work for I knew I could rely on him when it came to the brakes on the trolley, which he always handled with great care.

Then one day he disappeared. There were rumours that he had been caught helping someone and as a punishment was transferred to the coal mines in Westphalia where conditions were grim and where there were many casualties. I never knew the man's name or perhaps I just do not remember. I would love to thank him for his humanity.

As for the two SS women guards who had tried to send me away to my death, they finally realised that I was not going to denounce them. Henceforth I had no trouble from them. I think they thought that I was just stupid to have refused a good offer. I had more important things on my mind.

2 • Occupied territory

Before our arrival at the munitions factory as slave-labour, German workers, convicted criminals and foreign workers had been working at the plant. We began work with some German women and a German foreman.

A small organised group from our midst, former chemists, got themselves into the filling laboratory and, in order to minimise inspection, increased the production two and a half times. They enrolled a few additional persons – including myself – who were able, at various points of production, to do something unobtrusively to limit the effectiveness of the grenades. We became an organised sabotage group.

While I was working on the conveyor belt, my contribution consisted in leaving the caps loose on the grenades, instead of tightening them, as I was supposed to do. This I applied to grenades which had slipped through one or other of the sabotage processes. They were always marked so that the next in line knew if something had to be done to render the grenade ineffective. This depended on the inspection and supervision which became less and less frequent when the Germans saw how hard we worked and how much we had produced. The sabotage process went through the entire chain of production. In the filling room, some chemical element was omitted, sulphur for example. If the workers there were unable to cause damage as a result of strict supervision, a prearranged indication sign was passed on to the person next in line. Later, when I was working as a 'horse', offloading grenades, I was at the end of the sabotage chain. Any grenade left undamaged until the trolley stage was loaded in a way to ensure that the cap would split. After only a few days, we were so well organised that hardly a grenade got out of the building in which I worked which could have exploded. I never found out how many other prisoner groups sabotaged the war effort of the Germans in this way. If there were many, slave-labourers must have made a fair contribution in hastening the Germans' defeat.

Because of these activities, I resent the allegations that we Jews went like lambs to the slaughter. When Hungary was occupied by the Germans in March 1944, apart from a few exceptions, only Jewish women, children and old people were left to be taken into captivity. Normally, the men of military age and up to the age of 50 were drafted into the army. However, since Jews at the time were not allowed into the Hungarian Army, they were consigned to labour camps. They were often used as guinea-pigs to clear minefields and very few of them survived the war. Women in everyday life are not trained to defend themselves against armed men and as Jews we had no arms or ammunition.

In any event, by that time, March 1944, few believed that we would be occupied by the Germans. The invasion took Hungary completely by surprise. Many Jews committed suicide, because to stand up and fight was just not possible. We would have been mown down. The Germans used the so-called 'salami technique' in Hungary. They did not immediately take us from our homes to the extermination camp, but proceeded step by step. At every stage we thought that while it was bad, one could still put up with it, until we had nothing and were nothing, and suicide would have been the only means of escape from German tyranny.

As Hungary was the last country to be occupied by the Germans, we had already heard stories of German oppression. Refugees from all over Europe – French, Poles, Czechs, and Austrians among them – had sought asylum in Hungary. The Hungarians were very hospitable to all foreigners – but not to the indigenous Jewish population. Indeed, there were some 35,000 cases of Hungarian Jews being denounced to the German occupation authorities. Yet, before the Germans came, we did not quite believe the stories of their behaviour in other countries. It was the same after the war when many who asked me to tell them what happened to me could hardly believe what I told them. They did not think that I had lied but that I had exaggerated the facts. Even today, I sometimes feel the same reaction. It is understandable: decent people do not want to believe or to know that others submitted fellow human beings to such cruel treatment. It requires an incredible feat of imagination. March 1944 was almost the end of the war – or so we thought. In 1941 and 1942 we had expected Hungary to be occupied by the Germans but not in 1944. We all thought with relief that we had escaped the German yoke. And then, on 19 March 1944, the Nazis marched in.

At the time I was living in Budapest and I recall that it was a lovely Sunday morning. On Sundays, I used to go to a family to teach their son German and took the Number 16 tram on a pleasant route which skirted the Danube. After the lesson I returned by the same tram and it was then that I saw all the German tanks and military personnel. I realised that we were occupied. Not a shot was fired in defence or protest uttered except, as far as I know, in one single town, Sopron (Oedenburg in German) – on the Austrian border. My two great uncles (Uncle Béla and Uncle Zsiga Seligmann), fearing what would happen, committed suicide on that day without having communicated with each other. Both lived in Budapest on either side of the Danube.

That same day the Germans, with the help of the Hungarian Arrow-Cross fascists (the arrow-cross was the Hungarian equivalent of the swastika), began to swoop on the Jews, and within a few days the wearing of the yellow star was made compulsory for them. But at the same time something happened which greatly disturbed me and overshadowed even the arrival of the dreaded Germans.

To explain what happened I must go back in time.

After the *Anschluss* (the German annexation of Austria in 1938) I was taken out of school and, on the advice of the Austrian relatives, I had to learn a trade. This was considered more useful to me in case we had to emigrate from Hungary. I was placed in a milliner's workshop where I was apprenticed for the next two years. I loathed every minute of my apprenticeship.

The milliner to whom I was apprenticed was the mother of Edith, one of my schoolfriends. Edith was a pretty redhead and in school I was rather infatuated with her. (Oddly, when I was young I was always attracted to red-haired girls.) We were the same age but

23

Edith was much more mature than I. She and her parents perished in Auschwitz. Before I was apprenticed to Edith's mother I had quite liked her. But she proved to be a most unpleasant employer. I was a paying apprentice. At the same time working with me was another girl apprentice who came from a very poor family and who could not pay. She was treated very badly and I strongly resented this.

The milliner's establishment was the best in town. On the main square, it displayed a glass case in which every day a new hat was on show. The non-paying apprentice was required to wash that case every day. I felt that this was unjust and insisted that we take turns in performing the chore. Because her father could not pay for the apprenticeship that was no reason for her to be treated differently from myself. I came from a strong socialist background and my father was known as a very outspoken socialist who often addressed political meetings and published articles in the socialist press. But when I took my turn to wash the glass case my gesture was not at all appreciated in my very progressive home. My father did not think that it was right for his daughter to be seen on the main square cleaning a milliner's show-case. This greatly upset me. I felt that I was being reprimanded for practising socialism.

Indeed, I found practical socialism to be a very odd thing. Usually the same girl delivered the hats, but when she fell ill I was directed to take a hat to a client. When I was offered a tip by the customer I refused to accept it. I was brought up to think that working people should be paid properly and not be dependent on gratuities. Such a practice was immoral. Yet my fellow-apprentice was outraged when next she was sent to a good client and received no tip. She accused me of ruining her business. It was very difficult for me to reconcile theory with practice and I was quite baffled by this inconsistency. I was then between 15 and 17 years old, which might explain my confusion.

Meanwhile, my regular schooling was continued by my father every night for one hour. This was a highly interesting and fascinating experience, but spoiled by the fact that my father included my best friend Kati Kaufmann in his lessons. Kati was a brilliant student and had continued to attend school. My father was constantly comparing me with her. Having been treated most of my life

24

as one who was slightly stupid and slow, I felt that I was a disappointment to my brilliant father. I had no confidence in myself and my abilities and was basically terrified by my father and conscious of not fulfilling his expectations. Meanwhile I completed my apprenticeship, but resolved that in no circumstances would I become a milliner. I must confess that even today, I am a disappointment to my husband, who loves hats. Most hats suit me, but I refuse to wear them even to please him, so great is my aversion.

In 1942, against my father's wishes, I moved to Budapest. I was 18 years old and had always wanted to get away from my home-town, Szombathely, which I loathed. I also wanted to become a nursery school teacher and in spite of lacking the necessary qualifications, namely the Matura (roughly the equivalent of A-levels), I was accepted for teacher-training on the basis of an intelligence test. By that time, Jews were not admitted to state colleges but the Jewish community of Buda, which had an enlightened and highly intelligent rabbi, a psychologist, a paediatrician, an educationist and other outstanding Jewish teachers, had established a first-class paedagogical course for the training of nursery nurses and nursery school teachers. I was overjoyed to be accepted for study, since, from the age of 14, I would spend part of my summer vacation teaching German to children, with whom I loved working.

My father refused to support me financially, but after my mother had interceded on my behalf, he agreed to pay for my room only, nothing more. I would have to earn enough to pay the other expenses while I was engaged in a full-time course of study. I was always hard-working, though my father never acknowledged the fact and considered me stupid and lazy. I still cannot understand why he persisted in accusing me of being lazy, which was patently untrue. Admittedly my school results were somewhat erratic, largely because I could only learn from teachers I liked and for whom I had regard. My French, art and mathematics were rated as excellent because I respected those who taught them but my history studies were unsatisfactory because I intensely disliked the teacher who concentrated on the triumphs of Hitler's armies, was virulently anti-Semitic and altogether a thoroughly unpleasant specimen.

In Budapest, I supported myself by teaching German and French while doing a full-time course and preparing the very demanding homework at night, usually permitting myself only four hours' sleep. At the same time, I experienced the excitement of leaving a provincial town and living in a culturally exciting, lively and fascinating capital city. I went to theatres and concerts – the latter free – since as a student one soon learned the recognised sport of how to get into a concert hall without paying. I had a distant cousin who was a former student and knew all the tricks of the trade. He would tell me when he and his wife had purchased tickets or had a subscription for a series of concerts. Then I would arrive either alone or with other students and he would come out from the hall and give me his wife's ticket. She was already inside and so a chain was created via the two original tickets. The doorman at the concert hall already knew us and greeted us and I am quite sure that everybody accepted the ruse but closed their eyes to it benevolently.

I also sang in choirs. I could sight-read music faultlessly and my contralto voice seemed to appeal because whenever I auditioned for amateur or professional choirs I was invariably accepted. In a chamber choir led by a young conductor, András Kóródi (who later became well-known in Budapest), we sang madrigals and small works, old and modern. With another choir, conducted by Lichtenberg and nicknamed 'Bömbölde' ('a place to roar in'), we sang oratorios. Both were highly acclaimed choirs and I had a great time singing in them.

I did not eat very much in those days. I really could not afford full meals and my priorities were, I suppose, somewhat eccentric. The room which I occupied with Kati, my best friend, was on the top of a hill. At the bottom of the hill there was a large, round, glazed conservatory which contained the first espresso-bar in Budapest. Since the coffee there was very good and cheap, I was a frequent visitor. From the espresso-bar I went to my school which was on the next hill. At the bottom of this hill, there was August, a famous pastry shop whose Russian cream tart was my favourite. I had one slice every day and this was mainly what I lived on. Once a month I received a most welcome parcel of 'goodies' from my mother which I usually shared with friends or sometimes with just one special friend. And from time to time I was invited for a home meal by relatives or friends. Though not a very healthy life it was most enjoyable none the less.

One day I went to see my relatives at their imposing jewellery shop. My aunt was there and I was dressed in a nice grey costume. She gave me their newest creation, a very smart silver pin which served as a brooch. It was meant to be worn on the lapel of a costume and had a small aperture for a ribbon or small scarf to be inserted. The scarf was supposed to be of the same colour as the blouse one was wearing. A few days later, when in the evening I was going to the opera – I had been on the go the whole day – I wore my costume with a red blouse and a small red kerchief pulled through the pin. I noticed people staring at me on the tram and wherever I went. I could not understand why wearing a little brooch should attract so much attention. It was an odd sensation.

In the evening, at the opera-house, I met a friend from Szombathely. He was obviously pleased to see me but appeared to give me an admiring glance. He even told me how brave he considered me to be. I did not know what he was talking about. Then it dawned on me that it was the first of May and throughout the day I had been walking about with my red blouse and red kerchief. Communism was illegal in Hungary in 1942, but, of course, I had acted quite innocently. The next time I went home on holiday, I was greeted by my friends in the youth club with applause. They admired my courage in wearing a red ribbon in Budapest on May Day. My good friend had gossiped, in spite of my explanation that I was wearing red for no political reason. I tried to convince my friends that it was all a mistake. My protest was in vain; they would not believe me and thought that I was being modest about my courage in so openly displaying my devotion to socialism.

I graduated from college acquiring additional credits to teach languages and the recorder. One of the two directors, Dr Emmy Pickler, a renowned paediatrician, began to send me out on short-term assignments.

First I had to deal with two very disturbed children in my home-town, and, after several weeks, I managed to teach these poor rich children to play and to do things which weaned them from smoking cigarettes and compulsive listening to Beethoven's seventh symphony. Not a usual life for a five-year-old and a three-year-old who kept on screaming for hours if he wanted something! This involved unremitting work from seven o'clock in the morning until 10 or 11 at night.

After that job, I was sent to work under supervision in a summer-camp, where I learned a lot. Then to another problem child and to a private crèche with 18 infants aged between four weeks and four months – children whose parents had either neglected them or simply could not afford to care for them. I was on duty most nights and some mornings as well. As I was changing positions so frequently all on Dr Pickler's advice or at her direction – my father continued to maintain that I was lazy and could not keep a steady job. I rowed with him every time I returned home. He especially disliked my being away from home and, after heated arguments, I invariably left without saying good-bye. Such departures depressed and angered me.

The jobs to which I was sent took me through 1943. At the end of that year, I applied for work as an assistant in the model nursery school attached to my old training college, run by my favourite teacher, the joint director, Jenny Halász. Jenny was a hunchback and very neurotic but a wonderful human being and we got on extremely well. I respected the director of the college, Dr Pickler, but found her rather forbidding. But Jenny, I adored. So to be chosen among all those who had applied to work with her was for me the greatest honour. I was duly appointed and began jubilantly working at the nursery at the beginning of January 1944.

In February I suddenly fell ill with a high temperature every four days. On the fifth day, I would be completely fatigued, recover for the next two days, and then the fever would begin again.

At the time, I was living in a Jewish women's hostel, the Kurtág Piroska home, in the inner city on Veres Pálne Street. I resided there mainly because I had become friendly with two Czechoslovak girls, who, as it later turned out, were living in Hungary with forged papers; they had previously fled from Bratislava. We lived five to a room. As it was a hostel with a kosher kitchen there was little choice for meat or poultry. Beef was no longer being slaughtered according to Jewish ritual and chicken was much too expensive. The cheapest kosher poultry was goose, and so we lived on the bird, day in, day out. I did not know why I was unable to digest it, especially as I had a very healthy appetite and enjoyed eating goose. When my high fevers and other physical difficulties persisted, I consulted physicians who were distant relatives. After various examinations they wrote to my father and suggested that I should go to a sanatorium for thorough investigation. This upset me, for I loved my work and was fearful that the nursery would dismiss me if I was absent too often.

My father now wrote to me, after having received the letter from the physicians, asserting that it was obvious that again I could not keep a job and that apparently I was a hypochondriac. He absolutely refused to allow me to go to a sanatorium for investigations, insisting that he and another physician would give me the necessary examinations if I returned home. There seemed to be nothing else I could do in the circumstances and so dutifully I went home on Saturday, 11 March 1944.

During my journey home I had a high temperature but only the lassitude remained after my arrival. My father and Dr Heumann, our friend and family doctor, examined me and found nothing. And I did not even have a temperature. By the Wednesday they had decided that I was malingering, that there was nothing wrong with me and that I should return to my job. My father said I must return to Budapest the next day. My brother, who was in a labour camp, wrote that he could get week-end leave and would be back on Friday, 17 March. Even though my brother and I did not always get on, I still wanted to see him, as we had not seen each other for quite a long time. I therefore asked to stay and go back to Budapest on the Sunday. My father was adamant. Unless I left on the Thursday, he would not permit me to return at all. The result was a bitter row and I left home in the morning without saying good-bye. The date was Thursday, 16 March 1944.

Throughout the journey I was feverish and this time the temperature did not abate. On Sunday, 19 March, Hungary was occupied by the Germans. Three days later, I was taken to hospital and within a few days was operated on for a perforated colon. The day after surgery, Budapest was bombed by American planes; four days later the Germans threw us out of the Jewish hospital and took over its administration. My father had never permitted long-distance

29

telephone calls for, as he put it, one should think ahead and then one could write: only 'unorganised' minds needed to make long-distance calls, except in the direst emergency.

Now, he telephoned the surgeons in the hospital. He sent me money and messages asking me to forgive him. It affected me deeply. Practically every day there were messages from him. He even paid one of his patients to bring me money. He begged me to come home when I got better as proof positive that I had forgiven him for the way he had behaved towards me.

A non-Jewish young man, Mihály Szak, who was in love with me, came to the hospital with a friend, Egon Gráf, to bring me forged papers: they wanted to hide me from the Germans. I also had a message from a non-Jewish uncle, who wanted to hide me. Although I appreciated these offers of help, I refused, because I wanted to make peace with my father. No one knew what would happen to us and I had promised him to come home when I received the necessary permission from the authorities.

The permission came on the Saturday, 22 April, but with strict conditions. I had to wear, in addition to my yellow star which was sewn on all our clothing, a yellow armband. My permit was on yellow paper. In the train I was allowed to sit only if there was no-one sitting next to me. I was forbidden to speak to anyone and not permitted to use toilets or eat in the dining car. I telephoned my father telling him that I had permission to depart on the 24th, the day after my twentieth birthday. Father wept on the telephone and said we would celebrate my birthday a day later.

The journey lasted some twelve hours. We experienced an air-raid during which all passengers had to get out of the train and lie in a ditch alongside the track. I arrived in Szombathely a few minutes after six in the evening, carrying a suitcase and a violoncello – all my possessions. No Jew was permitted to be in the streets after six and no Jew was permitted to use the trams. By tram I would have had a five-minute journey. Without it, carrying the heavy suitcase and the cello, it took me some twenty minutes to reach home. During my walk, I counted 24 people who stopped me, asking how, as a Jewess, I dared to be in the street, spitting at me, calling me names. It was a journey which made it absolutely certain that I would never again be homesick for Hungary.

When I got to our home I entered through the kitchen. My mother was there, hardly acknowledging my coming. She seemed to have become an old woman – she was only 50 then – utterly dejected, and I could hardly get out of her the grim information that as soon as I had completed my telephone conversation with my father on the previous Saturday, German SS men and the Hungarian police had come and arrested him. They searched the entire flat. When I arrived, all its contents were strewn on the floor and the flat was in complete disorder. My mother was totally confused. She did not know where they had taken my father.

As I mentioned earlier, my father had been a socialist throughout his life and a very vocal one at that. He had written articles, lectured on the subject and had fearlessly aired his views in public. On the day they arrested him, they rounded up all politically suspect persons, Jews and non-Jews alike.

My mother was in a terrible state, a broken human being who needed looking after. At the beginning of May we had to leave our flat and move in with another family in a small room in the so-called ghetto. With Kati, my old friend with whom I had shared a room in Budapest, we collected all the Jewish children, and in the courtyard of the synagogue (luckily the weather was good) we looked after them during the day. At least the children did not have to be confined in the overcrowded quarters in which we were forced to live. Later, all those children and Kati perished in Auschwitz.

My mother and I were in the ghetto for seven weeks. We had no news of where my father had been taken. My mother was by now sinking into senility and in deep depression. I was sewing lunchbags with long handles in some of which I secreted people's jewellery. Although we were supposed to surrender all jewellery and valuables, most people retained a few things. By sewing these bags I earned a little money to purchase the few necessities which we could still obtain. At the end of June, we were taken to a disused factory which served as a concentration camp in which were confined some 4,000 Jews of our town and the surrounding smaller towns and villages. Many were beaten up by the police when jewels were found hidden on them. I threw away all the jewellery we had rather than risk being caught and roughed up.

31

The morning after we arrived in the camp, there was an order for 50 persons to go to a neighbouring town for work. I had decided that we had to go but, since Mother refused to move, I quite brutally forced her to come with me. Something possessed me to behave this way. When we arrived at the place of departure there were already 49 people in the group. I pushed an elderly woman aside to enable my mother and me to make up the numbers. Throughout the war this was the one deed of which I was greatly ashamed and which I regretted. But at the time, I just had to get into that group.

From the camp we were taken by train some 12½ miles to another disused factory. All warehouses or workshops were separated by wire fences. We were taken into one – and there was my father. It was wonderful and yet quite traumatic to feel his presence. The man who had always been so incredibly self-assured kept on pleading for forgiveness as he held my hand. As I recall, we were a couple of days in this camp and were then herded into railway cattle-trucks where we spent the next five days until we arrived at Auschwitz. Meanwhile, my mother became increasingly senile and finally went completely out of her mind. My father kept holding my hand, begging me to forgive him. I am convinced that the trauma of my personal situation made it easier for me to endure the madness, the deaths, the filth, the degradation and the misery of that journey. But I never regretted having returned home. The intuition which had driven me to join that particular group now seemed justified by fate.

There were only physicians, lawyers, and architects in the railway truck in which we were transported. The Germans and their Hungarian accomplices had crammed 120 persons into the cattle-truck, instead of their usual overcrowded 90. On our arrival at Auschwitz, my parents and I were separated from each other. My mother was immediately taken to the gas-chamber; I could never find out what had happened to my father. He was rumoured to have been seen in April 1945 in East Germany, but we never heard of him again. I was taken into Birkenau B Lager.

3 • Childhood memories

Szombathely-Steinamanger, a provincial town in Transdanubia, Hungary, was the place where I was born on 23 April 1924. It had some interesting sites and buildings, including the bishop's palace and the cathedral with the beautiful Maulpertsch ceiling. It was situated at the point where two Roman roads intersected, and the mosaics of the Roman basilica with fishes and other early symbols date from the time when the town was called Savaria, the capital of Pannonia, an important province of the Roman Empire.

In 1944 the town had some 45,000 inhabitants. Its Jewish population, with surrounding smaller communities, consisted of about 4,000 people. That was the number of Jews incarcerated in the so-called concentration camp, the disused factory where we sat on the dirty naked earth, clutching our bundles and awaiting further orders from the German occupiers.

My father, a gynaecologist, who also worked as a general practitioner, came originally from a small village in the Zala county. His mother was descended from a rabbi in Bohemia. His father was a timber merchant and manufacturer of concrete building components. As youngsters, when cycling through Zala county we were always pleased to see that all the culverts over the roadside ditches were inscribed with the initials M.H. for – we thought – Mosonyi Henrik, my grandfather's name. He was no longer alive when I was born and his second son Róbert was managing the by then rather run-down business. But it must still have been quite a going concern, for Uncle Róbert was the rich man of the family. My father's family also owned an attractive vineyard and orchard which my grandmother tended with loving care even when she was in her eighties, right up to the time when the German occupation began.

Fortunately, Grandmother was at the time in Budapest with her daughter, Aunt Vilma, who was married to quite a highly placed Christian gentleman, Uncle Miklós. They hid Grandmother for a while, until they were killed by a bomb, a direct hit on an air-raid shelter. No-one could look after Grandmother and so she went into the Budapest ghetto. She survived, but was so emaciated that she died soon after the war. I was very fond of this grandmother. She was a small, very bony lady, always busy. She lived in a large ground-floor corner house in the village of Zalaszentgrót. Uncle Róbert's office and the timber-yard were in her house and for a time this included a grocery shop run by a cousin. Inside the gateway there stood a black carriage used for family outings on special occasions.

The village was surrounded by fields of poppy and wheat and hills covered with vines. We spent many of our summer holidays in the vineyard. There was a very pleasant villa where one could live quite comfortably in the summer. The one problem was water. An ox-cart brought up the water several times a week. But when it rained the road to the villa was impassable and we had to sip wine from the cellar. Even as a child, I appreciated good wine.

I spent many holidays at my grandmother's, and she often came to stay with us in Szombathely. Zalaszentgrót, the village where she lived, was only 35 miles from our home and yet what a cumbersome journey it was to visit her! It took at least two, usually three, changes on the train; when I was older I would greet the stationmaster after the last change, hand the luggage to him to put on the train and walk the last two-and-a-half miles across the poppy-fields to my grandmother's house. It was quicker than waiting for the train, and later someone would go to the station to retrieve the suitcase.

As I have said, I loved this grandmother and I believe she was quite fond of me until one winter in my eleventh year when she stayed with us. One day we went for a walk. It was icy and Grandmother fell. I helped her to get up and I remember I was much upset and worried that she had hurt herself. But sadly at the same time I had a compulsive reaction which to this day I can only control with great difficulty: I can't help laughing when someone falls – even if I fall myself and am in pain. So I laughed when Grandmother fell and she never forgave me for it. From then on she believed that I was a heartless wicked girl. For many years after this episode I thought that her dislike of me was only in my imagination, but my impression was confirmed by Aunt Vilma's younger son, Róbert, who remembered that I was thought by the family to be a heartless girl and something of a black sheep. It still makes me sad that my grandmother did not understand that I meant no harm and that I really cared.

My father had studied medicine in Vienna and Berlin. At school he was an outstanding pupil and when he completed his Matura he was awarded a special prize of a gold watch and a holiday in Rome. He was also very musical, played the violin and the viola and gave talks on musical topics. When he had completed his medical studies and had specialised as a gynaecologist, the First World War broke out and he was granted a commission as a medical officer in the army of the Habsburg Monarchy. He served on several fronts including Bosnia-Herzegovina where he was wounded in action, and was transferred to the military hospital of Szombathely. When he recovered, Father worked in the hospital and also in the maternity clinic under the supervision of the director, Professor Reismann. After the war, the professor offered Father the opportunity to become his assistant. This is how he came to settle in Szombathely. During the war, in 1917, he married my mother who was brought up in Vienna. Her mother came from Budapest of a family of leading jewellers who served as Imperial and Royal purveyors in Hungary. My maternal grandmother had married her first cousin who lived in Vienna and owned a large removal firm.

My maternal grandfather was dead by the time I was born, so I never knew either of my grandfathers. My Viennese grandmother was a grand lady, always very elegant, formal and haughty. I did not like her. She had three daughters and three sons in that order. My mother was her youngest daughter. Mother had studied commercial subjects, English and stenography and later taught these subjects and German language in Szombathely. As a young girl she had been very much in love with a friend and colleague of my father who married a nurse, and so my father was her second choice. The thought of living in a Hungarian provincial town after Vienna did not appeal to her, and she persistently considered herself to have made a *mésalliance*. She was always resentful and bitter about her fate. Nevertheless, according to family accounts, the first few years of my parents' marriage were happy and loving.

My brother Pierre was born about a year after their marriage. He was a clever and very gifted little boy who used to hum Haydn symphonies before he could speak. As both my parents were very musical – Mother played the piano, though not well enough for my father's taste and therefore later never played but only listened to music – they were thrilled with their son. Being so happy with their first child, they decided to have another.

Unfortunately Mother had a very difficult birth with me and spent almost a year in hospital. Consequently a wet-nurse was engaged to feed and care for me. Apparently I was constantly screaming and it was only after some time that they realised that the wet-nurse did not have enough milk for both her child and myself. She kept me in short supply and I screamed because I was constantly hungry. No wonder my brother resented my presence. First of all, it was because of me that Mother was in hospital and did not come home. Instead, a bawling baby, demanding constant attention, was in the house. According to stories I was later told, he tried to do away with me a few times. I bear no grudge but even after nearly 70 years I am still not quite convinced he has got over his resentment. We meet only rarely, which is clearly all for the best, though it makes me very sad.

During the 18 years I lived at home, we changed apartments only once. The first flat was on the third floor of a building which stood on the corner of King Street and Queen Elisabeth Street. These were the two main streets of Szombathely, with King Street as the thoroughfare where people promenaded between six and seven in the evening on weekdays and on Sunday mornings. We schoolgirls walked arm in arm, often in groups, and boys also walked in groups, but we were never together. Of course, when one group passed the other and no teachers were in the offing some words would be exchanged, a forbidden and therefore exciting experience.

Our flat had a lovely balcony on the corner where I spent much

1   Dr Dezsö Mosonyi of Szombathely, the author's father

2   Dora Mosonyi, née Ullmann, the author's mother

3   Gertrud Mosonyi at the age of five

4   Gertrud Mosonyi aged nineteen – a year before the Nazis invaded
Hungary

time. At the entrance to the flat was my father's waiting room and the surgery, behind which was a long dark passage to the rest of the flat which consisted of three rooms, a kitchen and a bathroom.

Father was a health service physician. Patients could not choose their doctor and streets were allocated to each physician. Thus, Father was in charge of an adjacent street inhabited by religious Jews. Occasionally someone from this street became ill on Friday night or Saturday, and since there would be no one in the surgery, a bell connected the surgery to the rest of the flat to summon the physician. However, Orthodox Jews were forbidden to ring the bell on the Sabbath. When they required the doctor they banged on the door until they were heard. Often much hard banging was necessary, because either the radio was on or chamber music was being played in our flat. I never understood the logic behind all this. I should have thought that ringing the bell would have been much less in breach of the Sabbath laws than loud knocks since everything is permitted if there is danger to life.

I must have been about nine or ten years old when we moved next door into another flat which also had five rooms. My brother and I shared a room until I was about ten. From then on he had to sleep in the waiting room, which he resented very much and with good reason. The flat was well furnished. The sitting-dining room, which was also the room where my mother taught during the day, had elegant Biedermaier furniture. This also served as the music room. It was a beautiful room with good paintings. Except for two Abel Pann pictures I do not remember who the painters were, but I believe they were well-known Austrian artists. We also had some exquisite silver and some hand-painted porcelain for our dinner, tea, and coffee service, mainly gifts from my aunt's antique shop or from our jeweller family.

My parents' combined sitting-bedroom was very elegant and extremely modern. One of my father's patients was a joiner and cabinet-maker and he made all the furniture for this room in beautiful dark timber. When I was 16 years old he made for me some elegant 'bedsit' furniture with a built-in bookcase, bar and writing desk of which I was extremely proud. This was in preparation for my dowry. At the same time my mother purchased linen from Czechoslovakia, then sent it to Transylvania to be embroidered in preparation for it to be sewn together in our home-town. This was the world we lived in.

Today I find it difficult to believe that such a life existed. On the other hand when I was 15, my mother decided that I was no longer to have the services of the family's domestic help. I was henceforth required to do my own washing and ironing and to wax my parquet-floor every morning before going to school or later to work. As I was not very fond of housework, I usually spent my pocket money and privately earned money clandestinely paying the maids to do the work for me.

We had two servants: a chambermaid and a cook. A washer-woman came once a week to do the family laundry. Although the maids lived in, we had no special room for them to occupy. A small part of the kitchen was partitioned off with glass and curtains; this was where they shared a bed. They were not allowed to use our bathroom but had a bowl and a jug in their so-called room for their ablutions. Today I cannot understand how my parents, who prided themselves on being socialists, permitted two human beings to live in such conditions. Later in life, when I was in South Africa the servants had a room outside in the garden as they were not permitted to live in the house. But in their room they had some privacy, certainly much more than our servants had had in Hungary. And yet our domestics were relatively well paid in our service and had more free time than in other similar households. Our cook was with us for a very long time, actually until she married and my parents gave her away at her wedding. Her sister was for some time our chambermaid. But chambermaids changed often. As they had to open the door for father's surgery they had to look presentable and they had more contact with my father. The rapid turnover of maids was the result of my mother's jealousy of their close proximity to my father. The cook's mother often came to see her daughter and showed her appreciation by bringing from the country chickens and home-made cakes. As a child I sometimes went with Cook to visit her mother in the country.

Ours was a highly cultured home. We had some 3,000 volumes in our library in several languages: Hungarian, German, French and English, also some in Italian as well as in Latin and Greek from my father's student days. At home we spoke mostly German –

since Szombathely was near the Austrian border, it was the language which was once much in vogue, especially among the more educated folk. My parents were also fluent in French and English. As we had a world-renowned mental hospital in the town, English and American medical students and medical men and women of all nationalities came to Szombathely. A number visited us in our extremely open and hospitable home. During the Second World War, French and Polish prisoners of war, who had escaped from the Germans and found refuge in Hungary, enjoyed coming to our home for a chat with my parents or with myself.

We also had a large music library comprising scores, vocal and chamber music and piano music, since my brother was training to become a professional pianist. We had chamber music at home almost every week and both my father and my brother practised the violin, viola and piano regularly. Within the family we had innumerable singing sessions which I enjoyed immensely. Indeed, I grew up with French and German nursery songs followed by Schubert, Schumann and Brahms *Lieder* and Loewe ballads.

Music was an important constituent of Szombathely life. Musicians of older generations achieved considerable acclaim and in the 1930s and 1940s a young generation of musicians was maturing. Szombathely had a very active city orchestra of which my father was a regular member, playing the viola in the orchestra and either the violin or the viola when playing chamber music. When, in the late 1930s, Jews were banned from playing in the orchestra, the leading Jewish musicians formed their own orchestra called Collegium Musicum with Father as a founder member. Concerts were preceded by talks about the works to be performed, usually presented by Father, and were of a high standard. International artists came to play with the orchestra. I especially remember an occasion when a professor of the Music Academy, the pianist György Faragó, came to perform. He was not Jewish and had been warned not to play with a Jewish orchestra. Courageously, he took no heed and performed that night with distinction to the great delight of his audience.

My father's involvement with music went beyond playing in the orchestra and giving talks. He was one of the first to write about the psychology of music and produced a manuscript on the subject in

A Cat Called Adolf

German in the early 1930s. Unfortunately it could not be be published in Nazi Germany. He first approached Professor Sigmund Freud, the psychoanalyst, to write a preface. Freud replied that he had no understanding or enjoyment of music. Father then approached Romain Rolland who was very interested in the subject. He was an outstanding musicologist and professor of music at the Sorbonne in Paris, in addition to his literary fame, but he was unable to undertake the task because of ill-health and pressure of work. However, Rolland suggested his colleague, Charles Baudouin, who agreed to write the preface. An abbreviated version of the book was published in 1935 in Freud's journal the *Imago* (Vol. 21, No. 2). Since the Second World War some psychologists and musicologists have cited this article in their work (Desiderius Mosonyi, *Die irrationalen Grundlagen der Musik*) in France, in Germany and as recently as 1990 in the United States. My father revised the book and it was published in Hungary in 1934 under the title *A zene lelektana uj utakon*. A German version of the book, entitled *Psychologie der Musik* and edited by my brother, Pierre Mosonyi, was finally published in Germany in 1975.

This was the atmosphere in which we grew up. My brother was very gifted. He was outstanding at school, but his main ambition was to become a pianist. While still at school he spent all his free time practising the piano. He and Father had many battles, because Pierre wanted to stop schooling and concentrate on his musical studies. Although for Father, music was all-important, he did not think that a musician's career would bring security. He therefore wanted Pierre to finish his studies up to his matriculation (18 years) and perhaps study at university for a science degree. My brother did matriculate with excellent results, but then insisted on studying to become a professional pianist. During the last years of his schooling he had outgrown the local piano teachers and often travelled to study with well-known professors; first to Keszthely, to a cousin of our father, the pianist Mimi Mosonyi, then to Budapest, to study with Ilonka Vincze Krausz until her emigration to Palestine, and later with Agi Jambor, an outstanding pianist and teacher. He was 19 years old when he finally got to Budapest to study at the Music Academy where, after an audition, he was accepted by the director Ernö Dohnányi straight into the second year. Everybody

40

was elated and Pierre felt himself vindicated, for this was indeed a great honour. Sadly, it proved to be a mistake. Most of the pupils of the same grade were younger and had had the benefit of regular studies with excellent teachers; thus, technically they were much better prepared. It was an outstanding group of young students, most of whom became internationally celebrated pianists: Géza Anda, György Cziffra, Béla Síki, all Gentiles,[6] are some who spring to mind. Pierre was unable to keep up with them because of his very sporadic studies before coming to Budapest. He was demoted after the first year and although he was assigned to another excellent professor, Gyorgy Farago, it was a blow. Also, because he was Jewish, he was drafted into a labour camp, where he injured a finger while working in a mine. And so he was disappointed at not being able to reach his potential, which was a great pity. He was and still is an outstanding musician and coach and had the potential to become a top-ranking pianist.

I learnt to read and write quite early in my life and have always greatly enjoyed reading. Reading German or Hungarian was the same to me. I was left-handed, which got me into many difficulties when I went to school. I was continually caned on my hands for holding the pencil in the left hand. The result was that I became ambidextrous. I could never write neatly with my right hand and throughout my entire schooling I had trouble because of my bad writing. My drawing teacher thought that I was completely devoid of talent and hopeless. Much later when I was a milliner's apprentice I attended technical college where I had to do drawings. No one there cared which hand I used, and my sketches were acceptable to my instructors – indeed when I showed them to my former drawing teacher, she refused to believe that it was my work. However, being left-handed was only one of my drawbacks at school.

Another was my religion. My parents were atheists, but in Hungary atheism was illegal. One had to belong to one of the recognised religions and every breadwinner had a religious tax deducted from his earnings. Since we were Jewish we officially belonged to the Jewish community. According to the laws of Hungary, religion lessons at school were compulsory. I experienced great difficulty because I was unable to learn to read Hebrew. I had to take private tuition during an entire summer to pass my examination in Hebrew before the beginning of the new school year. Otherwise I would have had to repeat the entire previous school year.

The reason why I initially failed Hebrew was that I have never been able to learn anything from a teacher whom I dislike. I hated the religion teacher because he used to beat me and humiliate me in front of the class. The reason for this ill-treatment was my parents' atheism. Szombathely was a provincial town and it was accepted that the children spent the first four years in a Jewish school to be taught by Jewish teachers. During the first two years (aged six to eight) a nice elderly woman, Miss Friedrich, was my teacher. I was very fond of her and was a good pupil. In the third year, my teacher was a 60-year-old man who had no patience with small children and was extremely intolerant. He held it against me that my parents never went to synagogue and that my brother misbehaved at his religion classes. Thus my instructor had a double grudge against our irreverent family and vented his dislike on me. He beat me almost every day and treated me with utter contempt. I hated him and therefore could not learn anything from him. Worse still, the man was going to be my form-master in the fourth year as well! As we had a *numerus clausus* only a percentage of Jews were accepted in the Girls' Lyceum (equivalent to a grammar school) where I was supposed to go from the fifth year onwards; it was therefore most important that I achieve good results in the fourth year. To rid me of this teacher my father started a petition to force his retirement on the grounds that he was no longer suitable to teach young children.

The other parents agreed in principle, but when it came to signing the petition they demurred. My father then decided to take me away from the school and I was transferred for my last year in the junior school to a state school. Attendance at the school, which comprised largely working-class children, fitted in with my father's socialist ideas. But the main reason I was sent there was that the form-master was a musician friend of my father who had known me all my life and I was very fond of him. Since I was the only Jewish child among the 600 pupils in the school, I was still obliged to go back to my old school for religious tuition.

My new master, Mr Heinz, was an appalling teacher and taught us nothing. As I had a good voice and learned songs easily, he was very fond of me. But all I learned during that year was one song about a historical event, one song about Archimedes' principle and one song in geography. I came top of the class but had really learnt nothing. Otherwise it was an interesting year. Some children shunned me because I was Jewish. On the other hand I became extremely popular with the more deprived children in my class. The teacher chastised them on the smallest pretext with the cane and more often, by making them kneel in the corner on a hard, dried, seedless corn-cob, which was very painful. When I noticed that he did not punish me, I became a ringleader among my class-mates and thus saved them from punishments. I certainly must have made his life difficult.

At the other school, I had already experienced some trouble with some bullies because I always took the weak children under my protection. Since I was fearless and very much a tomboy, the bullies avoided me, knowing that I was a real fighter with fists, teeth and kicks, and I never accepted an injustice done to anyone.

Still I suffered much. In the new school I did not really belong. On the other hand at my old school, where I had to go three times a week for religion classes, I was ostracised by all the pupils. In winter I spent every afternoon at the ice-rink and became quite a skilled and enthusiastic skater. But that particular year my old schoolmates constantly attacked me and tripped me up while skating. I was always covered with bruises. I deeply resented my father's decision to transfer me to another school, especially since the old teacher had retired and the class now had a nice and highly intelligent young teacher.

The next year, having come top of my class, I was accepted at the Lyceum, but having learnt nothing during that year I was at a disadvantage with my classmates and had great difficulty in keeping up with them. Again I defended a girl everybody mocked against her detractors. Elly Blau was very bright but extremely fat and poor. She became one of my best friends and helped me with the class-work. No one dared to mock her when I was present. When she died a few years later I was most upset.

I spent five years at the Lyceum. Because I had a good alto voice, which was rather rare among the girls, I was accepted for the senior choir together with my friend, Claire, who later became a professional musician. As I spoke German fluently, I did not believe in learning grammar and soon got into hot water with my teacher whose spoken German was much worse than mine but who insisted on impeccable grounding in grammar.

I was blissfully happy with my French teacher, Miss Magda Szemzö, who was also our art teacher and who was one of the best teachers I had ever experienced. We all adored her. Nobody ever came to her class unprepared, because they felt it would have been letting her down. She was quite wonderful. At the end of the first year in a class of 45 girls, everybody was proficient in French. Miss Szemzö was Jewish-born, but her family had converted to Catholicism. She was a most devout Christian, unmarried and thinking of becoming a nun. Later, in spite of being a Christian, she was deported. We were together in captivity until the end of the war. She was the one who, in the camp, often upset me when she knelt in the hut to recite the Lord's Prayer. I found it rather galling that, as we were deported by Christians for being Jews, we should have to put up with this recitation in our midst. In 1970 I visited Magda in my home-town where she had returned after the war. She was no longer religious. By that time I had become more tolerant and understood that it had been her way of coping in the camp. I felt again the love and respect I had had for her at school.

I had a flair for mathematics and, although the teacher was an avowed anti-Semite, she tolerated me and even became fond of me because of my proficiency in the subject. Algebra fascinated me, but at the girls' school one only progressed to a certain level. I was so interested in the subject that later I continued to study mathematics privately. Today I am ashamed to relate that I have forgotten all I knew and cannot solve the simplest algebraic problem.

In chemistry and physics I did reasonably well, even though I was not much interested. In geography, I did quite well, but the continent of Asia eluded me. It looked amorphous on the map and I could make no sense of its vastness. Other places one could draw, for they had a shape. I preferred South to North America because it was easy to draw and therefore easy to remember, admittedly not very logical reasoning. And yet, in those days, I was considered to have an extremely logical mind for a girl.

Our history teacher was rabidly anti-Semitic. On the other hand,

I was extremely conscious and proud of being Jewish and I flaunted my Jewishness at every opportunity. The other Jewish girls deplored my conduct. They reasoned that because it was unfortunate enough to be born Jewish, it was best to keep quiet about it. For my part I felt that I wanted them to know that I did not mind being Jewish and accepted my heritage cheerfully. My history teacher wanted to humiliate Jews but knew that it wouldn't work as far as I was concerned. We disliked each other intensely. As a result, my history studies suffered badly, aggravated by the fact that I had had serious problems with the history teacher from the age of twelve.

At that time I was very much in love. The object of my infatuation was a youth at the boys' school next door whom I often saw on my way to or from school. I did not know him but I adored him from afar. My schoolmates often pulled my leg because I was terribly sensitive to being teased, and reacted by losing my temper. Obviously it was a sight they relished. One day, during the break before the history lesson, they whispered among themselves as I approached. Whether the news they imparted to me was true or false I shall never know, but I heard them whispering that Edith, my pretty school-friend, had met, the evening before, the object of my adoration and had spoken to him. I was devastated. I knew that if that were so, I would have no chance with the young man. At that point the bell rang for the history lesson. I returned to the classroom and poured out my sorrow on a piece of paper. Unfortunately, the history teacher caught me, snatched the note from me and read its contents out aloud to the class, much to my embarrassment. Then she sent me with the paper and her note to the headmistress who also wrote a note to my mother asking to see her. My mother came to the school and was informed about my 'highly immoral thoughts'. She acknowledged my guilt and as a punishment, she took away for a month my most cherished possession: a locked diary in which I daily recorded my innermost thoughts.

I could not understand why my mother did this to me and I never forgave her for this punitive act. From that moment onwards, I lost my love for her. Pity, yes, but no love. Even today I cannot understand her motives, even though she always maintained that she was a very advanced and modern pedagogue. I had done no wrong; not even according to school rules, which were very strict on boy–girl relationships. We were not permitted to speak to any young male on the street without the supervision of an adult. The school even had to approve attendance at a cinema. Parental approval was not sufficient. In most cases, even my parents deemed these regulations ridiculous. Later when we wanted to consort with boys, we would meet them in back streets or on the outskirts of town where we often cycled to spend the day with them, a practice which to my mind was much more dangerous than speaking to lads openly in the street.

After this day of alleged 'transgression' the history teacher constantly railed at me. On arrival in the class she would call my name and order me to stand up and recite the lesson. The day before a history lesson, I would spend the entire afternoon swotting but when called upon to deliver, I would be completely blank and unable to remember a thing. By that time she would be telling us about Hitler's greatness, a topic which certainly did not endear her to me. But I managed to get my own back. When, at the age of 15, I was taken away from school, I did a despicable thing which I do not regret even to this day. I persuaded a friend to find a dead rat, which I put into a lovely box tied with a pink ribbon. This was placed in a box with a blue ribbon and so on, five boxes altogether, and the entire package was posted anonymously to this most hated teacher.

When in 1970 I returned to Szombathely I learned that she had married the leading Nazi of our town and that she had behaved every bit as viciously as I had thought she would. Before that time I had some misgivings as to the veracity of my judgment of the woman, but now I felt vindicated.

A few years after the painful incident in the classroom, I met the Adonis whom I had worshipped from afar: he was a nice enough boy but certainly not worth the trouble I had incurred because of my infatuation for him.

4 • Anti-Semitism

Anti-Semitism was always rife in Hungary, and according to Jewish encyclopaedias, Szombathely was notorious as the most anti-Semitic town in the country. At school I had endured virulent anti-Semitism, and even earlier I had experienced anti-Jewish prejudice.

When I was a small child my father would take me for a walk on Sunday mornings, which I looked forward to with great pleasure. One Sunday – I was only five years old – my father told me that he wanted first to visit one of his patients before we began our stroll. As a gynaecologist, on the previous night he had assisted at a birth about which he was quite worried. He told me that he wanted to visit the mother to make sure that she was doing well. And so we went to a courtyard where very poor people lived. He left me standing outside while he saw his patient. Doors led from the courtyard into a large number of small dwellings. A door opened and then another and some children came out. When they saw me standing there, smartly dressed in a lovely red coat, they immediately began to call me 'dirty Jewish pig' and pelted me with stones. By the time my father came out I was bleeding and weeping. I did not understand why I had been attacked because I knew I was not dirty, nor was I a pig. A pig was an animal. What did the word Jewish mean? When Father explained about a people who were often hunted and not always tolerated in many lands, I declared I was going to be Jewish from then onward.

Although, as I have said, I was brought up in a household without religion, when I was about 13 I started to go through a religious phase, though it lasted only about a year and a half. To this day I remain an unbeliever and indeed, since the war, I have become a confirmed atheist.

Szombathely certainly lived up to its anti-Semitic reputation. In

1941 when Hungary was not yet occupied by the Third Reich, German troops passed through the town on their way to Yugoslavia. I remember well the dismay among the Jews at the thought that we had been occupied by the Germans. It was Good Friday and suddenly the entire main square – we lived on its edge – was full of German tanks and armed German soldiers. It was really terrifying. I was then about 16 years old and in love with a very handsome Christian student. Alas, I soon found that he was pro-Nazi, and that was the end of my first great love. I vented my disappointment in a poem, but very soon got over my sadness. The German units remained in Szombathely for three days; it was a foretaste of the occupation in 1944. No Jews were permitted on the streets after six in the evening and quite a few who ventured out were assaulted.

Following the departure of the Germans, there was unrest and one anti-Jewish restriction remained that was unique even in Hungary: Jews were permitted to go to the market (which was on the main square) only after ten in the morning, when everything of good quality had been sold and there was little, if any, choice for purchasers. As far as I know no other town had similar regulations. In Szombathely – so I had been told – almost everybody had joined the fascist Arrow-Cross Party. When later we were occupied by the Germans and the Jews were hunted down as undesirables, no-one, not one of our regular non-Jewish lifelong friends who used to come to dinner at our house, helped us in any way.

To some old friends we gave a few possessions to keep for us until our hoped-for return from captivity. Fortunately, at that time my brother was away from Szombathely. Indeed, he was the only one of our family to return to the town after the war. Only one person, Elly Kuzmanek, did not deny having some of our possessions. And she was not even a very close friend but the wife of the mayor, who was himself a socialist like my father. She was the only human being in a town of 45,000 inhabitants who behaved in a decent way towards us.

Before the war, as far as I can remember, I was extremely trusting, but the experience with friends – or those we thought were friends – left deep wounds and a permanent scar. Today, I would still like to trust people, but deep down I do not because I am often suspicious when there is no real reason to be wary. It makes

48

me sad. It was not only the so-called friends in Szombathely who made me so suspicious. The behaviour of co-inmates in the camp added to these feelings of mistrust which still, though less and less often nowadays, cause me to question trusting people, wondering how they would react under adverse conditions. Yet I have many friends and do my best to reciprocate with loyalty and affection.

During 1970 my husband and I, on a motoring trip, found ourselves not far from my native town. Dr Heumann, our closest family friend and general practitioner who managed to survive the war and returned to Szombathely, was then 80 years old. Before the war he, Uncle Laci as I then called him, was a bachelor, but after the war he married a friend of my mother who also managed to survive but whose husband perished. My French and art teacher, Magda Szemzö, who was with me during the entire war and who returned to Szombathely, also lived in the same house as Dr Heumann. We visited them and spent four hours together. I rewarded my husband for taking me to Szombathely by taking him to Ják, my favourite childhood place, some 7½ miles away from town. There was a superb Romanesque church we often cycled to when we were youngsters. We also viewed the local Roman excavations.

Although all this was attractive, the return to Szombathely made me physically ill following the night of our visit. I now felt that I never wanted to return there. I could not forgive the people for the way they had behaved when we were taken away to the concentration camp. Not a piece of bread was given to us. They knew my father who gave his staunch socialist beliefs practical application by charging very little for his services. In fact, he was so generous that there was always a shortage of money at home. As a gynaecologist, he could have built up a flourishing private practice and earned much money. Abortion was illegal, but gynaecologists usually performed this service for a large fee. My father performed abortions only if he felt that the social circumstances of the patient warranted it and then for no fee.

We always had enough food of good quality. Food in Hungary was abundant and cheap. The peasants and other patients brought us chickens, eggs, home-made butter, cream and sour cream. My grandmother sent us fruit from her orchard and vineyard. Vegetables were very cheap and since we had a very varied kitchen we ate extremely well. Flour and sugar were also very cheap and so was good-quality meat. Whenever we went to visit my mother's family in Vienna, though they were affluent, we took prime beef fillet with us for their table. Hungarian oxen were fed on sugar-beet and Hungarian beef was reputed to be the best in the entire former Habsburg Empire.

Most of the money my parents earned went on books. My mother supplemented our income by giving private tuition in German and English. She was also the treasurer of the Jewish Women's Group and, unlike my father, a Zionist. My father never joined the Zionists. There was always a bit of a problem when it came to purchasing stockings or some new item for my mother or the household. And there were many complaints that the rent for the flat was too high. Many other medical practitioners had cars; my father went everywhere on his bicycle in his old leather jacket. Even at night, when he had to go to distant villages, he travelled on his bicycle. Only when there was a snowstorm did he hire a carriage to take him to his patients.

There was little or no money for travelling. For holidays my parents would either visit their relatives in Vienna or spend their time in Grandmother's vineyard, living very frugally. Every four or five years they would take their rucksacks and go mountain-climbing in the Dolomites, staying in mountain huts which cost little. Family finances were further strained because they supported my brother while he was studying at the Budapest Music Academy until he was conscripted for labour service.

Whether it was out of principle or because the family was hard-pressed for money, I always had much less pocket money than my friends. As I had my own needs to attend to, I began at an early age to earn money during the holidays. I helped out at a stationer's and then at a haberdasher's. When I was 14 I worked half a day throughout the summer looking after two children and teaching them German. I really enjoyed teaching and seemed to possess some skill tutoring. At that time, it was the fashion to wear big peasant skirts with a wide oilcloth or leather belt. As the oilcloth belt cost more than my whole month's pocket money, I bought oilcloth by the yard and a buckle and made a belt for myself. They knew me in the shop where I bought the material and when I showed them my handiwork, they asked me to make some belts for them to sell. Since there was always a spare triangle of material left over, I made replicas of lizards, birds and other creatures from these bits and put a pin on them, knick-knacks which the shop also purchased from me. At the same time I discovered a liquid with which I could make drawing paper transparent to simulate parchment. I also made bookmarks with raffia, lampshades and imitation flowers.

In the summer that I was 15, I met a girl from Budapest, Jutka Heimler, who was on holiday in Szombathely. We developed a doll out of wire which we then dressed up in various clothes. These dolls we could bend to sit, stand and ski in all sorts of poses. We earned quite a bit of money in this venture. She invited me to spend my next holiday with her in Budapest and I paid for my journey and all the presents and entertainments involved in my stay. For the first time I went to a good theatre and to the opera and to concerts with professional orchestras.

I shall never forget the concert with the world-renowned Dutch conductor, Willem Mengelberg – it was really exhilarating – which I attended with my brother and his friend, the only time that I remember doing something really enjoyable with my big brother. At the time we were unaware of Mengelberg's pro-Nazi feelings. After the war he died in disgrace in Switzerland. While we were at the concert, it began to snow and when we came out everything was an ethereal white. As we walked home from the concert hall, Budapest looked like a jewel with the lights on the freshly covered snow. Not for nothing was the city called 'the Pearl of the Danube'. I had enough money to go every night to some event; it was a most exciting holiday. Since the war I have often wondered who was carrying on making our wire dolls, as I saw them again first in Israel and later in many countries.

From the age of nine I was a member of the Zionist movement and remained an active member until I left Szombathely to study in Budapest in 1942. I was a member of Hashomer Hatzair, a Zionist socialist group. After the war, I discovered that it was Moscow-orientated and felt that I could no longer belong to the organisation. I did not rejoin it because by that time I had heard of the Stalinist purges and had no sympathy for Moscow-type Marxist socialism. I had also lost all my idealism and did not believe any movement was worth my allegiance. I have never since joined a political movement.

In the anti-Semitic environment in which I grew up, the idea of a Jewish state very much appealed to me. I wanted to go to Palestine and to be part of the Jewish homeland. At the time the Zionist Movement was illegal in Hungary. When I grew older I became a group leader in Hashomer Hatzair. I remember that when I went to the opening of the hall of a newly organised group in Sopron and I was standing with the flag, singing the Hatikvah (the Jewish national anthem), the police arrived, took us to the police station and kept us there for a couple of hours. It was my first encounter with the law. I do not remember how we were set free, but I do recall that we thought we were very brave and regarded the whole thing as a big joke.

In December 1941, Hungary declared war on Britain, the USA and the USSR. In a last-minute effort, those who had emigration papers at the British Embassy were granted visas and emigrated to Palestine. I had also applied to emigrate to Palestine but I lacked one document and therefore could not join the group. Later, I tried to emigrate illegally and was again unsuccessful.

At the same time my mother attempted to get permission to go to the United States with me. Father refused to leave Hungary; he regarded himself as first and foremost Hungarian and was convinced that the Hungarians would protect him. When, in 1942, he received an official letter requesting him to return his war medals and was informed that he could no longer consider himself a Hungarian, he was devastated. His entire world fell apart. Shortly afterwards, a series of laws against the Jews were promulgated which further discriminated against him. Father had by then been employed by the railways, the post office and the general health service. The railways were the first to offer him continued employment, but on condition that he convert to Roman Catholicism. He refused because he could not accept any religion and convert for profit's sake, and thus he lost his job. His colleague, who had always reproached us for not practising the Jewish religion, converted with his entire family. From then on that unfortunate man was ostracised by the Jews, not accepted by his Christian colleagues and kept his job only a few months longer than my father. He and his family were later deported to Auschwitz extermination camp and never heard of again. My father had at least kept his self-respect.

But Mother wanted to leave Hungary and insisted that I must go with her. She had applied for an American visa as a native-born Austrian some time previously. It was granted and arrived in the post just a few days after Hungary declared war against the USA. It was too late; we were unable to take our place in the American quota of emigrants assigned to Austria. Poor Mother! When the First World War broke out she had been in England as an *au pair* studying English. She had returned on the last train from London to the Continent. She had loved England and always pined to return one day. In the summer of 1939 she had finally managed to put aside sufficient money to go to England for a university refresher course. Again, war intervened and she was compelled to return on the last train to Hungary. Had she stayed in England, she would in all likelihood have survived the war.

My mother was not a happy person. Her married life after my birth was not very good. My father was a womaniser and she was terribly jealous and in time became quite paranoid about him. She told me all about her predicament from the time I was 11; I loathed this family problem which often erupted in terrible rows between my parents. I did not want to know or to be burdened with this unhappy situation and disliked my father for making my mother so unhappy.

Every night when I went to bed my mother would come and kiss me. While I was a small child she would bring a sweet or a chocolate as a last thought for the night. (Very unhealthy, but oddly enough my teeth were always excellent and I never had a filling – until after the war as result of starvation.) Emotionally, such affection did me the world of good. It was a sign of love and caring in a very unsure and uneven emotional family environment. One night when I was about 12 my parents had a terrible row which greatly upset me at bedtime. I waited for my goodnight kiss for a long time, but mother never came. Very much later, my father came and kissed me. I felt that there was something very wrong and cried myself to sleep. The next morning, the maid woke me up early and told me that I was to go with her to the hospital where my father had been taken during the night. He had attempted suicide and had injected himself with 40 grammes of morphine. My mother had woken and, hearing his unusually heavy breathing, called an ambulance. He recovered, but had jaundice for the next six months. Another time Mother took an overdose of aspirin, but that was not very serious as it seemed more a device to frighten my father. In general, it was not a happy home and as a result I was always anxious to get away from the family as soon as possible.

And yet, in spite of this unsettled family situation I have some fond memories of my life at that time: the walks in the fields, with my father explaining all the botanical wonders, plants and healing herbs, observing ants working, frogs' eggs, and bird life, and the trips to the mountains – still one of my favourite pleasures – to pick berries and mushrooms and plants from which we made a fragrant punch. I learned to make flutes from willow reeds, to weave baskets and to eat roots. We looked at stones and trees and landscapes, spent much time in the orchard and vineyard where Grandmother dried pears, plums and apples and made very good wine. And we sang and read much. From very early on in my childhood, I accepted my father's guidance for my reading and never lacked literary matter. I also enjoyed cataloguing our entire library of over 3,000 books.

Father built a large wireless with batteries and earphones for everyone to use and enjoy. When an opera was broadcast we sat with textbooks and scores and followed it from beginning to end. The following day we would take the score or the piano version and play and sing it through again; in this way I got to know many a great operatic work even before seeing it staged. What I enjoyed most were the chamber-music evenings. I would have loved to participate and very much wanted to play the piano, but as my brother was preparing to be a professional pianist and practised some eight hours a day, I did not get a chance to learn. My parents decided that I should learn to play the cello, but at the time there was no cello-teacher in the town. Subsequently, a teacher was found who was prepared to come to Szombathely once a month, until he managed to build up a practice with several pupils. At nine

54

years old I was the first girl ever to play the cello in my home-town. But whenever I went to my lessons carrying my cello, children would run after me and call me names. Grown-up men would stop me and tease me with such remarks as: 'Big cello where are you taking this little girl?' And they would pinch my cheeks. I was so upset by these taunts and jibes that at times I even disliked my instrument. Yet at the same time I felt proud to be doing something that no one else in town had attempted to do – for a girl to play the cello!

Birthdays were the only dates we really celebrated. For my mother's birthday we would always prepare a musical offering with songs and poems – often written by my father or later by myself. Sometimes my brother set the words to music. When I began to learn the cello, it was decided that we would play one movement of a Mozart Piano Trio. I was very proud of being included in the ensemble, but it was much too difficult for me. Both my brother and my father would criticise me and every practice session would end with my leaving in tears. Finally, they did manage to get me to play my part. I dread to think how it must have sounded. Emotionally it was a very expensive birthday present.

As I was quite musical and a pretty little girl with rosy cheeks, my cello teacher made use of me in an attempt to get more pupils. I never learned a scale or an exercise from him. He taught me to play pieces, some quite difficult, and every time there was a student recital, I was put on stage and performed like a little monkey. But as I had no knowledge of basics, I had no idea of what I was doing. Later I managed to play a little chamber-music with other young people and very soon my father took me to play with him in the adult orchestra. A few years ago I met someone from Szombathely who had been an amateur violinist in the same orchestra. I was amused when he told me how very badly I had played and how the other members of the orchestra had resented my presence. Yet, at the time, I was very proud to be one of their number.

Later, when I lived in Budapest, I began to take lessons with a first-class cello teacher, but I had very little time to practise. Then the war came. After the war, for a long time I had no cello, until my first husband bought an instrument for me in Durban, South Africa. Then again I had no money to take lessons. However, when

I was again living in Durban, from 1951 to 1957 (before we came to England), I played with a regular chamber-ensemble and in the Durban amateur orchestra. But I never advanced from the last desk in the cello section, as I had neither teacher nor time and money simultaneously to take lessons.

5 • *Survival and disillusion*

I have survived and the general assumption is that for the survivor normal life again resumes at the end of the ordeal. How far indeed this is from the truth in the majority of cases and my own in particular!

On that awful Death March I collapsed and was left lying in the road near the river Elbe at a village called Klingenhain. The guards decided it was not worth putting a bullet into me in my emaciated wretched condition. In Germany everything was disintegrating.

It was 23 April 1945 and my 21st birthday. I could not get up. I had dysentery, I was starving and extremely weak. I managed to crawl away from the road into a nearby farm stable. After a while a young German woman came into the stable, probably to feed the animals. When she saw me she told me that it was too dangerous a place for me to remain as there were still German soldiers around. She directed me to a barn where I could hide and gave me a small piece of bread. With great difficulty I managed to crawl to the barn where I hid in the hay. I heard some Hungarian spoken and recognised the voices of two of my former camp inmates, a mother and a daughter. The daughter was the child to whom I had sometimes brought soup when I volunteered for some job in camp. They were exhausted and could go no further.

At nightfall some men came into the barn with torches and knives and a revolver. They spoke Russian. Since I had picked up a few words of Russian I explained, though it was hardly necessary, who we were. They were Russian prisoners-of-war who had been maltreated by German farmers who had now gone into hiding. These Russians were trying to find them. Instead they had found us. At first one of them wanted sex with us, but he quickly realised that we were only skin and bone and unappetising creatures. And so they went off but soon returned with an officer who spoke German. Shortly afterwards, they brought some stretchers and took us to a farm. They had formed a patrol but the Russian Army was on the other side of the Elbe at a place called Strehla. They were staying the night to hunt Germans, but at six o'clock in the morning they had to report across the river to their Red Army unit. As we were Hungarians, they would take us with them, they said, and later see that we were repatriated to Hungary. Though my friends were pleased at this prospect, I was not. I was suffering from partial amnesia, but I did know one thing: on no account did I want to return to Hungary. And so I hid in the straw during the night, and when they were looking for me I kept quiet. I knew that they had to leave on time and that if they did not find me they would have to depart without me. Although I did not know what would happen next, I had made up my mind not to fall into the hands of the Red Army.

After the Russians had left, I crawled out of my hiding-place. Later I heard French being spoken in the courtyard. I managed to get nearer and called out to the men, who were ten former prisoners-of-war. They told me that a liberation centre had been opened by the Americans some 18 miles away at a place called Wurzen. They were going there to be repatriated to France and they invited me to go with them. But when they realised I was in no state to walk, one of them offered to stay with me and look after me until I could get on my feet again. His name was Charles Oreste Paroldo, from Toulon, and he had been a prisoner-of-war for almost five years. All this came about because I spoke fluent French, which I had learned at home and at school.

French was always my favourite language. One of my mother's sisters had married a Frenchman by the name of Gaston Vidie, who became my godfather. They had no children and there was some talk in the family that at the age of 15 I might go to Paris to live with them. France was the place where every leading Hungarian writer and poet had at some time lived or visited and Hungarian literature was full of French themes and places. As a child I would listen to French spoken on the radio as though I were listening to music. France was the country of my dreams. My mother, who had lived a year before the First World War with an English Quaker family, was extremely anglophile. But I was in love with French and everything connected with France. The French films with Jean Gabin, Louis Jouvet, Michel Simon, Sacha Guitry, Michèle Morgan, Marie Dea, Françoise Rosay, and many others which we saw until 1942 were considered by us the best films ever made. They were indeed classics and were especially appealing since they combined romanticism with the ideas of Liberty, Equality and Fraternity.

Charles was a simple, intelligent but not very well-educated man. He nursed me and fed me and looked after me with kindness and tenderness. In my experience, during the war in the concentration camp, people of his type behaved much better than the sophisticated intellectuals among whom I grew up. I was therefore quite overwhelmed by this young Frenchman's concern for me and fell deeply in love with him. He said he had fallen in love with me and asked me to accompany him to France where he would marry me. I was delighted. To be alive, to be in love, to go to my beloved France, what more could I wish for?

By 29 April I had managed to get on my feet and we started walking slowly. We were in luck. A tractor came along flying, of all things, a French flag, and pulling an open truck full of people, all French. There were 38 people on board. They took us with them and we arrived in Wurzen where, because we were an organised group of 40 people with transport, we were issued with passes and permits to requisition food and lodging on our journey to the French border at Metz. There were eleven women in our group all former concentration camp inmates, and we were the very first survivors to enter France. Charles vouched for me, saying that I was his fiancée and that we were going to his home in Toulon to get married. We were issued with clothes, food and money and were fêted with bands at every stop. It was marvellous. And we were in love. That was even more marvellous! We stayed in Paris for three days and I was so deliriously happy I did not even remember that I had an uncle there. I subsequently found out that I had been only one street away from him and his wife! (His previous wife, my aunt, had been run over and killed by a bus in 1935, but he had always kept in touch with our family.) We stopped again in Lyons and more clothes and money were lavished on me. Finally we arrived in Toulon on 11 May 1945.

At Toulon we were received at the station by the Red Cross. We were questioned closely and again Charles explained how we had met and that he had brought me to France because he wanted to marry me and would accept responsibility for me. But as he had been away for five years and anticipated that it would shock his family to see him after such a long absence, he suggested that it might be better if he went home first on his own and then returned to fetch me. And so he left me with the Red Cross officials who listened to the story of my life since leaving Hungary.

It was now almost three weeks from the time that Charles had found me until our arrival in Toulon. From just over six stone which I weighed at the time of my rescue, my weight had more than doubled. As a result of starvation, followed by normal eating, I had developed an anaemic condition which had caused me to become greatly overweight. I had always had a red-cheeked healthy complexion, and now in France I did not look as if I had been starved or emaciated. Moreover, what was to cause me so much trouble was the fact that, unlike other refugees from concentration camps, I was not tattooed. As I explained earlier, when, on 2 August 1944 we were being prepared for transfer from Auschwitz to the Hessisch-Lichtenau camp and the SS guards began to tattoo our group, an air-raid occurred and, as all lights were extinguished, the tattooing was halted, with only some 20 or so of our group being subjected to the process. In that air-raid, the adjoining I.G. Farben factory which was producing Zyklon-B for the gas-chambers, was bombed by the American Air Force. We were transferred to Hessisch-Lichtenau with numbers sewn on our clothing but without numbers tattooed on our forearms.

Charles did not return to the Red Cross station to fetch me. I was devastated. The Red Cross people consoled me and finally sent someone who located him. He apologised for the delay and took me home with him. His home consisted of rooms on the third floor of a building in a very poor district. The small kitchen was divided by a curtain behind which was a bowl for ablutions and two buckets for other purposes which, when full, were emptied through the window into the courtyard. Charles's mother accepted me with something less than enthusiasm, and I had to share a bed with his very beautiful 16-year-old sister. But my devotion to Charles was such that even this depressing environment did not discourage me. Following my arrival, I did not see Charles for four days. Meanwhile I helped his mother to wash and clean the flat and pick some vegetables from their allotment. In the evening the mother, the daughter, and I went down to the nearby harbour to a brightly lit open-air dance-floor. The clientele consisted of sailors of all colours. In Charles's absence his mother and sister urged me to dance and drink, but I had no wish to do either. I took my betrothal and forthcoming marriage to Charles very seriously and did not want to enjoy myself without him. While we were at the port dance arena the girl and her mother would disappear from time to time and I was pestered by men to consort with them. I was extremely naive and innocent and it took me a couple of days before I realised what was required of me and where the mother and daughter went when they disappeared, leaving me on my own.

I realised that this was no life for me and I demanded to know where Charles was, refusing to eat or make myself agreeable until I could speak to him. On the fifth day after my arrival they produced him. He was very apologetic, saying that he had so many things to do. I now asked him to take me back to the railway station to the Red Cross people where I could seek employment. As I spoke French and was a qualified nursery nurse and nursery school teacher, surely I could get a job with their help.

Charles promised me that he would do what I asked but said that it would be advisable to go dressed in my Buchenwald shirt and jacket. Meanwhile, I could leave my other possessions at home. When I found employment and moved somewhere else, he would bring what I had left with him. On our arrival at the railway station, he asked me to wait outside while he went in to see if the Red Cross people were there. A few minutes later he returned with two policemen who put handcuffs on me and, after handling me roughly, locked me in a dirty cell in the police station. I never saw Charles or the possessions I had left with him again. I was penniless and had only the clothes on my back – my blue and grey striped concentration camp jacket and my grey sleeveless flannel shirt.

The cell contained a chair and nothing else. I sat utterly bewildered, unable to understand what had happened to me. It seemed as if the world around me had collapsed. Somehow my whole life appeared to flash before my eyes and my disillusionment with humanity was so great that I felt I did not want to live any more. With a piece of broken glass I found on the cell floor I cut my wrist (I still have a small scar from nearly 50 years ago). Before I had managed to sever an artery (the glass was thick and not very sharp), I was taken before a policeman for interrogation. The shock of what had happened to me seemed to have lifted my amnesia. I suddenly remembered the uncle in Paris, my aunts in New York and in Lausanne and the name of a French slave worker, Paul Morell from Bordeaux, with whom I had worked while offloading the grenades at the munitions factory in Fuerstenhagen near Hessisch-Lichtenau.

The policeman told me that Charles had told the police I was really an ex-SS woman from Germany and should be locked up with the other SS women and their French and Italian collaborators. I told him that the accusation was false and gave him the names of all the people I could remember so that he could check out my true identity. He promised to seek verification of my story, but in the meantime I was to be transferred for three weeks to the prison camp at Bandol and then sent to Marseilles for confinement in the Prison St. Pierre. The fact that I was imprisoned with French *miliciennes* (fascist women) as well as Italian fascist and German SS women was so incredible that it made me feel absolutely drained. And yet, of those terrible three weeks in Bandol which followed, I remember only three things: that the prison camp was at the top of a hill overlooking the beautiful Mediterranean sea; that I had an inordinate craving for onions, which I had never before experienced and which I would consume as if they were apples. Supposedly I lacked iron. Finally I remember that I spoke only to the staff and tried to avoid speaking to any of the prisoners. I have no memory of what my quarters were like.

Things took a turn for the worse at the prison in Marseilles, to which I was taken three weeks later. When I arrived there I was told by the police that they had had replies from most of the persons whose names I had given to them and it was obvious that I was telling the truth. In principle, they could set me free, but in fact they could not, because my file had not arrived from Toulon. Toulon is in the Department of Var while Marseilles is in the Department of

Bouches du Rhône: two different administrations. My file did not come. The other prisoners all had their own clothes and had money with which to bribe the guards to take them to the beach to bathe and to purchase decent food. I had no money and ate only the greasy, heavy prison fare, which other inmates avoided. But I could eat to my heart's content. From the age of 15 I had been a heavy smoker but now could only obtain or cadge an occasional cigarette. So to compensate for my tobacco craving, I ate all I could stuff into myself. Yet I was constantly hungry. It seemed as if my body was trying to make up for its long starvation and deprivation.

In the rat-infested room where I was confined there were 42 women, each assigned to a bed. Three languages were spoken: French, German and Italian. Some tried to make friends with me and slowly I responded to two of them. One was a 17-year-old girl whose father had volunteered to work in Germany and had taken his 15-year-old daughter with him. She had been arrested with her father and imprisoned. I accepted her friendship because I felt that she had been wrongly incarcerated. She was a kind-hearted girl who was horrified by my story. The other was a half-Jewish German woman (or so she claimed), but I do not recall why she was imprisoned. After my release I never saw any of these women again. But my 'liberation' still took some time. In spite of my concentration camp experience and my very first love-affair with a man, for which I was having to pay the consequences, I was still extremely naive. At first I could not understand the untouched beds and the women who slept together. They were lesbians and for me it was a completely new aspect of life which at the time I found repulsive.

One of our policewoman guards became quite a friend. She was the only one who believed my story and she tried to help me. I shall never forget Bastille Day, the Fourteenth of July, when I was in prison. It had always been my dream to spend that day in France and to take part in the celebrations. But here I was on this celebrated day, in 1945, crying my eyes out not knowing how long I would have to endure unjust captivity with hostile strangers. I told the policewoman of my sorrows as we heard the singing, the music and the dancing outside. I could not sleep. At midnight my dear policewoman (I wish I had not forgotten her name!) came to my bed

63

and told me to get up very quietly and follow her. She took me out of the cell and sat me down to feast on a large plate of fruit and sweets and cakes which she had brought for me together with a small French tricolour. I was deeply touched and kept this very kind gesture a personal secret.

I remained in prison for four months and still the all-important file did not arrive. Someone from the social welfare department of the Jewish community in Marseilles came to see me to ask me if I knew the *Shema* (the Hebrew confession of faith) and if I was really Jewish. Then one day in October I had a very bad toothache – during this period I had lost several teeth through prolonged malnutrition – and the friendly policewoman escorted me to the local hospital to see a dentist. As I sat in the waiting-room, hand-cuffed, in walked two men, one on crutches, the other his escort. I recognised the one on crutches. He was the man who had given me the Buchenwald jacket in a camp called Tekla near Leipzig on 7 April 1945.

Who was this man? I have to digress from my narrative. We had been taken from Hessisch-Lichtenau as the Americans approached the camp. Since before Christmas we had been listening to the guns and bombardments which we understood were near Kassel, some twelve miles from camp. We thought we would soon be liberated. At the time, I had one of my uncanny premonitions and was almost lynched when I said that we were only going to be freed on 23 April – although I was not sure if I would still be alive by then. To my astonishment my premonition came true.

In March 1945, we were about to be transported to Buchenwald to be liquidated in the gas chambers, but our captors did not reckon on the strafing accuracy of the American low-flying aircraft. They destroyed the engine of the train in which we were being trans-ported to Buchenwald, leaving the wagons undamaged. It took another three days for another engine to arrive. By that time the Americans had liberated Buchenwald and we were taken to a camp in Leipzig, which until a few days previously had been an SS camp and seemed to us unbelievably civilised. Hungarian women from another camp had preceded us and their German commandant was now in charge of the former SS camp. They told us how good their commandant had been to them, how he had seen to it that nobody had to work too hard, how they had always had clean clothing and warm water in which to wash and had been provided with adequate rations. Compared with our emaciated group, they were in extremely good shape. At this new camp we had our first marvellous meal since being confined and hot showers, clean bunks and bed linen. We were just resting after our meal when an air-raid began.

The Americans must have believed they were bombing SS personnel. Within minutes the entire camp was destroyed. My best friend – a lovely girl whose name I no longer remember – panicked during the bombing and to calm and comfort her, I got off my bunk and lay down next to her holding her hand. Within a second, her head was split in two by shrapnel. It was terrible. Her sister, who was lying next to us, started shrieking. I lifted the body and ran through the bombardment to the medical hut, even though I felt that it was in vain. She was dead in my arms. I only had on a sleeveless flannel shirt and it was very cold.

Later, from the ashes and debris, I miraculously retrieved my scrapbook, the pages of which I had accumulated during my time in Hessisch-Lichtenau and strung together into a booklet. I had noted down songs and poems which we sang and recited so that I could maintain some smattering of culture in my memory. This was my only and most treasured belonging. (Unfortunately, at some point of the Death March, I lost this precious volume.) In the late afternoon we were taken to another camp, marching through the ruins of Leipzig. The part of the city through which we walked was gutted as a result of that afternoon's bombing. It was an odd sensation – to be touched at seeing such a great city in ruins and yet elated at a death blow to Nazi tyranny. Indeed, the bombardment had thrilled me. I felt it did not really matter whether I survived, the main thing was that the Germans were being vanquished and the end of the war was near.

The camp we were now taken to was called Tekla. It was a camp for men, though we were separated from them by barbed wire fences. But I managed to make contact with a French inmate who had come from Buchenwald. He provided me with a Buchenwald jacket and got me a piece of soap. Next day we started on the Death March. There were thousands of us, most in very poor physical condition. It was snowing and very cold. Anyone who fell was shot on the spot by the German guards. We marched in ranks of five. Unfortunately, the five people who were my closest friends, Luciana, the two Czech girls Hedva and Éva and Grete Wurzel, were in the row behind me. At some point on the edge of a forest on the second or third day of the march the entire row broke up. Luciana managed to slip away with one of the Czech twins and did not know that the others also had slipped out. I could not follow them. A whole row of five was not so conspicuous but to leave four would have meant endangering my companions. I suppose I also lacked the courage to remain on my own in case I could not find the others. Shortly afterwards we heard shots in the forest and we were told that those who had attempted to escape had been shot. This was not true, for they all managed to survive. Every time we halted, my French benefactor, the one who had given me the jacket, appeared, each time in a worse state, to see if I was still alive. We received nothing to eat during the march, but I found a raw potato and somehow managed to slice it into twelve parts, six of us having two slices each.

By the fifth day my Frenchman failed to appear. On the evening of the ninth day of the march we were escorted over a bridge across the Elbe at a place called Strehla. During the march, we had to take turns at pulling the baggage wagons containing the belongings of the SS guards. Meanwhile, the guards put on Buchenwald jackets over their uniforms in an attempt to disguise their identity from the low-flying planes which dived down on us. In Strehla we were herded into an open area where we settled down on the ground for the night and were given a handful of raw rice. A horse was slaughtered to provide raw horsemeat for us to eat. This was the first food we had had on the Death March. In this camp, on the other side of the Elbe, the dive-bombers were Russian.

The guards now seemed to have decided that they preferred to fall into the hands of the Americans rather than the Russians, and next morning they marched us back over the bridge. There was a sunrise the like of which I had never seen in my life. It was so beautiful. We dragged ourselves over the bridge and then I collapsed. It was 23 April 1945, my twenty-first birthday.

Now, months later, in the Marseilles hospital waiting-room, I recognised the man on crutches as the Frenchman who had given me the jacket and the soap. When I requested permission from the kind policewoman to ask this man a question, she wondered why I wanted to speak to him, but after slight persuasion she assented. When I asked him if he had ever been in a camp called Tekla near Leipzig, he looked at me in wonder and exclaimed 'Gertrud, what are you doing here and why are you handcuffed?' It was then obvious to the policewoman that he knew me and this was one more piece of evidence that I had been telling the truth. We both told him what had happened to me and why I was imprisoned. He was in a convalescent camp for deportees and said that I must not worry, they would see to it that the authorities would set me free very soon; he would substantiate the truth of my story.

That afternoon a dozen men in Buchenwald jackets came to the prison and presented a magnificent food parcel to me. And the next morning 50 of them came to speak to the prison officer. They then went to Toulon to see the prefect who had refused to transfer my file to Marseilles – the reason why I was still in prison after four months. His refusal to transfer the files had something to do with his having lost his two sons in the Resistance movement, and he could not be convinced of my innocence. The delegation returned by noon and I was released. They took me to the Chamoins-les-Bains convalescent home, a superb hotel set in exquisite gardens, housing deportees. During the German occupation it had been the local Nazi headquarters. Once again I was free. The official who had delayed my liberation was, I was informed, dismissed from his post.

6 • Work, study and Stephan

We arrived at the convalescent home for lunch, which consisted of a good French meal, all the more palatable after the stodgy prison food. I had a room of my own. There was a bowl of fruit on the table with flowers and some clothes for me to try on. I was in the seventh heaven. Although I was told that I could remain for a while, I wanted to get back to normal life. As soon as he knew that I was alive, my French uncle and his wife invited me to join them in Paris and I was keen to take up their invitation. I was much too impatient to sit and do nothing after the past four months of enforced idleness. I also wanted to go to Paris to see at first hand the city of my dreams.

During the same afternoon I was trying on the clothes I had been given, there was a knock on the door and was told that my cousin had come to see me. I said I knew nothing of a cousin, but when I was finally persuaded to open the door there to my amazement was my favourite cousin Gucki. I could hardly believe my eyes.

Gucki's mother was my mother's eldest sister. Aunt Lili was my favourite aunt. A large woman with a beautiful face and laughing eyes, she was a marvellous raconteur, even though she had a reputation for mixing true stories with fantasy and was often unable to differentiate between fact and fiction. She herself believed the stories and for me as a child they always seemed convincing and colourful. Aunt Lili, who lived in Vienna, married an antique dealer, Uncle Rudolf, and had three sons. As she had always wanted to have a daughter, I spent many holidays with her. Aunt Lili and her family were affluent. They lived in an apartment with fine furniture and paintings. I liked spending time in their shop which was round the corner from their flat. I was much taken with the various pieces of furniture, some with hidden drawers which I spent hours trying to find. My uncle was the president of the Austrian Antique Dealers' Association and my aunt used to loan furniture to the Josefstaedter Theatre when it staged period pieces. By the time I was eleven she was also involved in staging plays there, or so I was given to understand. Through her I met Austrian acting celebrities, among them Gisella Werbezirk, and was able to augment my autograph collection of which I was very proud. Aunt Lili also had a fine villa on the outskirts of Vienna at Moedling. The house was surrounded by a large and attractive garden with tortoises I loved to play with. The villa seemed to me to be like a picture-book castle with high mansard windows. I particularly loved the two superb and extremely beautiful tiled stoves in the corners of two rooms. I believe that after the war they were taken apart, tile by tile, by the Russians; they were certainly not there when the first survivor of the family later returned to the villa.

Aunt Lili was the only person who ever spoiled me, though I made it hard for her to do so. She often took me to a large store in Vienna's Mariahilfer Strasse which contained only dolls, three or four floors of dolls, dressed in outfits for every occasion, with small suitcases for travel and sports clothes and dolls' houses. I found the collection fascinating in spite of the fact that at home I never played with dolls. My poor aunt could never understand this. What I really wanted was a teddy-bear, but I never had one. Aunt Lili bought me dolls. The first one she gave me cried and so I cut open its tummy to see where the sound came from. The second doll moved its eyes and was beautiful, but I scalped it to see how the eyes moved. The third one was supposed to be unbreakable, but when I threw it down from the third floor to test it, it proved mortal. Following these experiences Aunt Lili gave up buying dolls for me. I loved to play with my brother's Matador or Meccano sets and to create things out of bits of discarded materials. I also loved to watch my father mend the electric iron or the typewriter or anything that needed repairing. It was a most unusual hobby for a Hungarian professional man which others of his standing usually considered beneath their dignity.

I was not especially fond of Uncle Rudolf. He and Aunt Lili often quarrelled loudly and I found these rows most disquieting, feeling sure that my dear aunt did not deserve such abuse. When the shouting matches made me cry, Uncle Rudolf would give me a present to pacify me. These presents certainly pleased me, since I was an inveterate collector. In addition to my main hobby, autographs, I collected cosmetic samples, soaps in all shapes and colours, tiny tubes of toothpaste, and small flasks of perfume. My French aunt sent me some of these samples, and I spent most of the last holiday I had in Vienna before the *Anschluss* in 1938 going to drugstores begging cosmetic samples which were easily obtained. (On the Continent chemists do not sell soaps or cosmetics. These are sold in separate shops which, for convenience, I call drugstores.) My guide and guardian was my cousin Gucki, the youngest son of Lili and Rudolf. Nothing was too much trouble for him as we wandered together endlessly from shop to shop. In between these excursions he took me to the Prater, the local fairground, to see the puppet show; the next morning he would present me with linocut pictures and ink-drawings of all the puppets. Gucki was four years older than I and a most delightful person. I often fondly recalled his kindness to me in those far-off days. The last time I remember seeing him before the war was in 1936. Now here he was at my door.

After the *Anschluss*, Gucki managed to get to Palestine where he joined the British Army. At the end of the war he went to Italy, still with the British forces, and it was there that he heard of my plight. He managed to get a few days' leave, 'organised' a jeep, got papers for me and came with loads of cigarettes and other good things to get me out of prison. Arriving an hour after my release, he followed me to Chamoins-les-Bains. I spent the next few days with him gorging doughnuts in the NAAFI. He tried to persuade me to return to Italy with him to a refugee camp near where he was stationed, but I was determined to go to my beloved Paris, so Gucki returned to Italy without me.

I stayed three weeks in the convalescent home in Marseilles and felt very spoiled. It was a most enjoyable place, where I met a number of people who were kind to me. One nice American Jewish soldier even wanted to marry me, but all I wanted was to get to Paris. I arrived there some time in October.

My uncle, Gaston Vidie, was a real Frenchman and an inveterate Bohemian who did not believe in working unless he felt like it. In

1945 he was 62 years old. His wife, Maud, aged 35, accepted me with kindness. They lived, it seemed to me, an odd life. They had no children but had two small, spindly-legged, squeaky black dogs (out of the original seven). These were their babies. At the time this was beyond my understanding, and I was hard put to it to conceal my dislike of these funny undersized animals. Gaston was quite good-looking, with a cigarette perpetually dangling from his mouth. At one time he sold some disused aeroplanes to the Chinese, having previously run an import-export business with the Americans as his principal customers. He had once owned a racecourse in Casablanca. In the early 1930s Gaston had produced a film with nude actors, including himself and Aunt Emmy, which was considered much too pornographic even for the libertarian French! In the 1960s, his widow was approached for rights to the film and she received some much-needed royalties for permitting its showing. He had published a book called *Amoureux de la mort* (*In love with death*), and whenever there was an essay competition in the newspapers, he would enter and often won first prize. The Vidies would spend the prize money by inviting all of their writer and actor friends to a champagne and caviare dinner. Then they would revert to their customary penury. Lacking funds for food, they would stay in bed with the dogs, a coffee percolator at their side. A kind friend would bring them a loaf of bread and the newspapers until some money was again earned or obtained.

The Vidies lived in a gloomy ground-floor flat filled with interesting antiques and curios (most of them erotic) from all over the world, and most in a rather dirty condition. They had very little, but what they possessed they offered to share with me. I greatly enjoyed the oddness of it all and my uncle's witty conversation. It must have been quite difficult for Maud, who was Gaston's fourth wife. I know nothing of the first two, but the flat was full of photographs of the third wife, who was my real aunt. Gaston had always kept in contact with our family and was as helpful as he could be to his many Jewish nephews who found their way to Paris during the war. Maud did not seem to resent Gaston's generosity and cheerfully supported him in all he did for his relatives.

I was grateful to the Vidies and sought to show my gratitude by some deed. In my innocence (perhaps stupidity) I began to clean the flat thoroughly. Although my uncle appreciated my efforts, Maud felt that it was a reproach to her. Consequently our relationship became strained. I was upset and as I was seeking employment to earn my living, I accepted the very first job offered to me. It was an unfortunate choice, but it got me out of the Vidie household. As soon as I had left them, Maud once again became friendly, helpful and supportive. This friendship lasted until her death some 30 years after that of my uncle in the 1960s.

The job I obtained was with the Women's International Zionist Organisation (WIZO). I was put in charge of a children's home in Montmorency, a town near Paris, and was paid a very small salary in addition to full board and lodging. I was also promised one full day and two evenings off a week and, after a few weeks, some help with the cleaning. A social worker was to supervise my activities and provide the home with all it required.

The children's home was a large two-storey house with some ten rooms, originally the home of two elderly French women. During the war they concealed and looked after 40 Jewish children between the ages of two and 14. The parents of these children were all deported and only one of them ever returned. The father of one boy, the eldest child in the home, was a German SS officer, who came to visit his child even during the war. It was said that the mother, a French Jewess, had been deported at the instigation of her German husband. When I arrived at the home there was no soap, very little food and no heating. For a bath, we had to take the children to a public bath-house. Two women had looked after the children all through the war. One did the cooking and the other the washing and some cleaning. Though very strict, they were extremely kind to the children. Unfortunately, they deeply resented my supervisory role at the home, which now with hindsight I can appreciate. It was really an insensitive thing to do to send a 21-year-old girl to take charge of the home. But at the time the woman made life extremely difficult for me. The children were very disturbed and the boy with the German father constantly wanted me to assure him that the Germans were not all that bad. I did the best I could. Though there were usually five to eight children in sick-bay we lacked the services of a doctor and the necessary medicines. During the night I slept with the children in the sick-room and in the morning I had to see that the elder children got to school on time, clean and adequately dressed. In the afternoon I supervised their homework. In addition to these duties I conducted a nursery group for the smaller children and tried to clean the house. Six weeks passed and I had not had one minute off. No social worker came. The two women I worked with became ever more resentful of my presence and even of my name. I was still called by my full name, Gertrud, which the Frenchwomen found too Germanic and proceeded to call me Germaine. Since Germaine meant German I found this quite amusing. I myself disliked the name Gertrud. I did not like Germaine any better, but it did not much matter.

Every time I telephoned WIZO headquarters I got only promises of relief and assistance. Although desperately tired, I continued to put on weight. Finally I decided to confront the people in charge of the home and was on my way to Paris when I collapsed in the street. This misfortune finally moved WIZO to send a young girl to help clean the house. She was 16 years old, had not the slightest desire to work and was far more a hindrance than a help. Once again I collapsed from exhaustion and, on the physician's advice (he diagnosed acute anaemia), I had to stop working. For the next six months I was treated with injections three times a week in an effort to restore my health and to deal with a heart condition.

When I was in Marseilles, I had been given the address of a French Jewess, Berthe Douet (now Berthe Ghersin), who was my age and lived in Paris. Her parents had a market stall there, spoke Yiddish and had hearts of gold. They were not well off and lived very modestly. They had three daughters. The eldest, Berthe, was married to a Frenchman who had saved her life during the war. She had many friends, and as I only had a permit to work with children but was not in a fit state to do so, Berthe helped me to get another job. My employer was a weaver with one loom and my task was to work eight hours a day preparing bobbins for him. Since I was now employed illegally, the pay was poor. I did not mind the work, but other favours were expected, and when he would not keep his hands off me I was obliged to leave.

The next job I obtained was quite an advance. This time, it was a weaver whose entire workshop of looms and bobbins was electrically operated. My job was to watch the bobbins and, when a thread broke, to tie a knot. I was not very good at this because my reactions were too slow and so this job did not last very long.

Meanwhile, I had been accepted – as a concentration camp survivor – as a mature student for study at the Sorbonne. I wanted to study psycho-paedagogy and was accepted for an excellent course conducted by Professor Henri Wallon. I also studied history of music, aesthetics and analysis under Professor Paul-Marie Masson. But at the same time I had to earn a living. I was offered employment at the Hungarian House (a social and cultural centre), working in the office, addressing envelopes and doing other trivial duties. The job meant working from two o'clock in the afternoon until midnight, five days a week, and although badly paid, it at least helped me to subsist.

As I had a good voice, every choir for which I auditioned took me on, even illegally, during my stay in any country. Thus in Paris I became a member of two choirs. One was at the synagogue on the Rue de la Victoire under the noted choirmaster, Leon Algazi, every Friday night and Saturdays and on festivals. The other choir was in Neuilly; we sang, under the direction of Jacques Berlinski, at weddings and special occasions and on the radio in a programme entitled 'La Voix d'Israel'. In both choirs I worked illegally and consequently was paid less than the other choristers. But it all helped.

Unfortunately I was unable to attend Professor Wallon's lectures because they were in the afternoon when I had to work. On the other hand, Professor Masson's lectures were not of a very high standard: he had little regard for any composers other than French. We studied Rameau's treatise on harmony which was Professor Masson's speciality, and as a concession, Belgian-born César Franck, whom he regarded as an honorary French composer. We spent two years analysing Franck's violin and piano sonata. But to Mozart and Bach only one lesson was devoted and to Beethoven none at all. I did get to know Mehul, of whom I had never previously heard and, during the ensuing 45 years, have encountered only once.

While working with the weavers I ate in a canteen run by the American (Jewish) Joint Distribution Committee, better known as the JOINT. Since my adventure with Charles, I was wary of every man I met. So I never accepted invitations to go out with men and even refused to let any of them buy me a cup of coffee. I lived on the fifth floor of a shabby hotel in the Rue St. Denis. I was quite friendly with the concierge but knew none of the inhabitants.

In the canteen, a Polish refugee often sat next to me. He frequently asked me out, but I always declined his invitations. He was an intelligent young man and we talked a lot. One day we discussed a book I had just read. He wanted to read it and I promised to lend it to him. He accompanied me to my hotel. When we got there he came up to my room. I quickly gave him the book and sent him away immediately. I did not even offer him a chair to sit down on, so afraid was I of any male attachment. Five minutes after he left there was a knock on the door. A handsome Frenchman asked if he could come in. When I asked what he wanted, he explained that he was one of the French prisoners-of-war who had escaped from Germany and had found refuge in Hungary. He said that he had been in Szombathely and asked if I remembered him, since my family was so kind to him and his colleagues and had invited him into our home. It had come to his knowledge that I was in Paris and he wanted to call on me to talk of old times. I was very moved by what he said because I remembered the French and Polish prisoners. My parents provided hospitality to many Frenchmen during 1942–43 when they were refugees working in a factory in our town. So I let him into the room and the very next minute he grabbed hold of me and attempted to have sex with me. I was outraged at his conduct and threw him out.

When I next came past the concierge's lodge, she told me that I had been very lucky. The man was from the French police vice squad and, as I had let another man come up to my room, he sought to find out whether I was a prostitute. I never found out how he knew about my background and if he had really been in Szombathely and at our home. I was completely shattered when, as a result of this unfortunate experience, I discovered that the hotel was mainly used by whores for their business. I moved out the next day and henceforth was even more frightened and careful about meeting men.

Next door to the canteen the Neuilly choir often practised. One day I decided to join it, not knowing that it was a professional choir. I got an audition with Jacques Berlinski, the conductor, was accepted and pleased that I was to augment my meagre earnings. One day, when I arrived for a rehearsal, I found that it had been cancelled, but Berlinski was there. He had not notified me – so he said – for he wanted me to meet a Hungarian violinist friend of his. This was Stephan Deak. He was tall, with a good head of dark hair, and was quite handsome.

When I was living in Budapest from 1942 to 1944, I was frequently at concerts, singing in choirs or in the company of musicians. Music was essential to me and has always formed an important part of my life. Most of my friends were musicians, and Stephan had either made their acquaintance or knew of them. He was Jewish, though that was not very important to me at the time, he spoke Hungarian and knew the literature and the poems I grew up with and loved. So we had things in common. He had also lost almost all his family, and now had only a sister living in Hungary. He had not been in a concentration camp but had spent many months in hiding. At the time we met he was also destitute and in pretty bad shape. I was alone and Stephan stirred a maternal instinct in me. Here was I struggling to earn enough to pay for my miserable room and to support a very modest existence, and here was someone who shared my interests and who was even worse off than I. I had been brought up to respect music and musicians who deserved every support and in no circumstances must endanger their hands with menial work. In Stephan Deak I had found a cause and now I thought I was in love.

My first real love had been for a cellist whom I had met when I was 17, when I was playing in the Jewish Orchestra, Collegium Musicum, in Szombathely. We were having our break during the dress rehearsal and were waiting for the soloist to arrive. When he entered and came through the hall, I was standing beside my cello and he came up to me and greeted me as a cellist colleague. I was overjoyed. And then we began to play the Boccherini B flat major Cello Concerto and when he struck his opening chord I somehow felt he was playing for me alone. I was so deeply affected by the music's incredible beauty that tears rolled down my cheeks. I have heard many great musicians since childhood, but never have I ex-

5   Charles Oreste Paroldo, the man who 'rescued' Trude and took
     her to France in 1945

6   October 1945, Chamoins-les-Bains: Trude with her Viennese
     cousin Gucki Berger (left), who came to take her to Italy

7   Paris, June 1946: Marriage to Stephan Deak

perienced such deep emotion as on this occasion. It was love at first sight (or perhaps first hearing) and it was reciprocated. During the following days every minute we could steal from our work we spent together. Then my loved one returned to Budapest and we exchanged at least one letter daily and often two or three. He dedicated a small work to me, composed using the letters of my name. I also managed that year to go to Budapest and we were in the seventh heaven. Holding hands, we walked through the Fisherman's Bastion, one of Budapest's most romantic and glamorous places. It was all completely innocent. I also organised a solo recital for him in our town, despite the strong opposition of the Music Society, and filled the hall to overflowing.

Then the letters suddenly stopped. I did not understand why, until one day, a letter came from his mother telling me to leave him alone and implying that I was a dangerous seductress! I was devastated, and could not understand how he could allow himself to be so much under his mother's thumb. The scar remained until healed by Charles's kindness and humanity in taking me to France after the war. But then Charles had me put into prison and robbed me of what little I had. It took a great deal to get over this trauma and disillusion.

And then I met Stephan. The tone of his violin or viola playing was exquisite, but his style, musical taste and technique were rather questionable. As he had achieved the highest diplomas both as an academic and as a virtuoso, I attributed his defects to his war experience and to what he had endured during those terrible years. Before the war, I was often requested to be present when some of my friends were practising and was asked my opinion of their playing; I was told that I had a good sense of style, though I myself could hardly be called a cello expert. I started working with Stephan when he practised and this compensated me for the tedium of my office work at the time. There were other reasons why Stephan and I came together. We attended the same study course at the Sorbonne, and last, but by no means least, he was not aggressive like all the other men I had met up till then.

When I saw his studio, I should have run away from the disarray I encountered. But instead I cleaned it up and put his music and his clothes and all of his belongings in order. Eventually, even though he had no income and what I earned was hardly enough to keep me alive, we decided to marry. But to marry we needed official papers, which I lacked. Without a birth certificate it was not possible to tie the knot. Our entire existence was hampered by the lack of proper documents. Neither of us had a work-permit and I had no passport and was stateless. And so Stephan moved into the hotel room in which I lived. One room was certainly cheaper than two. The hotel was in the Rue des Blancs Manteaux in the Jewish quarter of Paris.

7 • Marriage

The room in the hotel on the top, fifth floor, was light and quite a reasonable size compared with other cheap hotel rooms in Paris. One of its serious defects was the mice. We had a mousetrap in every corner, and almost every evening when we returned home the traps were full. But one gets used to many things and we were quite happy. Stephan was trying to get engagements. As he lacked a work permit, the only employment he could obtain was playing at Jewish weddings or other special festivities, which were very rare occurrences. One day he ventured to join a Hungarian Gypsy band, which paid extremely well, but did not continue with the group as he considered it beneath his dignity to play with them. I understood this, for my upbringing was such that it did not seem right for a classical musician to play Gypsy airs or other light music. Today, I have overcome such prejudice and now realise how silly I was to entertain such a notion. Next to the hotel there was a small grocery store where I went once a month to buy everything we could afford to purchase on our rations. I hardly ever bought anything but basic foods for we were extremely poor. The next shop in the street was a Hungarian bakery, where, on rare occasions, I had a brief chat with the owner. When our papers finally arrived and the day for our wedding was set, my uncle offered to arrange a small reception with a few friends at his home after the marriage at the register office. An old friend of my Aunt Lili, whom I visited sometimes, gave me a pretty pale blue dress of hers to wear and someone else provided a pair of stockings. Another friend even bought some flowers for Stephan to give me as we had no money for such niceties.

We did not take the wedding all that seriously, for we were already living together. But when I told my baker that I was getting married, he offered to bake a cake if I would prepare it, and gave me extra flour to make it. And so I made the round of pharmacies until I had collected sufficient poppy-seed which the baker had promised to grind for me. I went to the pharmacies because in France poppy-seed is considered as being opium and a poison and can therefore be purchased only in minute quantity, certainly not enough to fill a poppy-seed cake of Hungarian proportions. Having completed this task, I went to the little grocery shop to buy some raisins and nuts. The woman in the shop – we had never spoken before – was surprised by my request for such luxuries. She asked what the special occasion was and I told her that Stephan and I were getting married and that I was baking a wedding cake. She asked me where we came from, where our parents were, etc. As I prepared to leave, she asked me to do her a favour and pop in for a moment in about an hour.

When I returned she told me that she and her family were Russian Jews and, having spoken to some of her friends, they had decided that, as we had no parents, they would make a wedding for us. They had already hired a hall and now proposed to invite ten of our friends for a special dinner. This was most touching and, after some hesitation, Stephan and I accepted the offer. We went to the place the following evening. The hall and a horseshoe table were decorated with flowers. There were present some thirty Russian Jews and our friends who fêted us with toasts and a very good meal. It really was very moving. And then a rabbi appeared and the hosts brought a tray of golden rings from which I chose one that fitted. A *chupa* (canopy) was erected and Stephan and I were wed according to Jewish rites. We were somewhat embarrassed by the proceedings because we were not religious and regarded the wedding ceremony as rather a joke. When the glass on which Stephan had to stamp did not break the first time, he asked jocularly (in Hungarian) who would pay for the repair of his shoes! After signing the *ketubah* (marriage contract) we were given presents by all the Russian Jews. It was indeed heart-warming and, although we did not take it very seriously, we were deeply grateful for such kindness.

The following day I went to the shop to say 'thank you'. Unfortunately, the second day after our wedding, our room was burgled and all the presents which had been given to us by the Russians disappeared, but oddly not those from our own friends. A few days later I went to the grocery shop and found it closed and empty. The people had gone, and we never saw any one of the thirty Russians who had fêted us again. Quite a while later, when for the first time, I had decided to divorce Stephan, I went to the offices of the Paris Chief Rabbinate and found that the *ketubah* and our religious wedding had never been registered. Were it not for the testimony of our friends who attended the wedding (my friend Berthe still remembers it today), I would think that it was all a fantasy.

Stephan wept throughout our wedding night and for the first time I became aware that much more was wrong with him than depression as a result of being a refugee.

At this time, the local Jewish students' union had organised the first post-war International Jewish Students' congress at a place called Uriage-les-Bains, near Grenoble. Since Stephan and I were members of the union, they offered us a week's holiday at the congress if Stephan would agree to play for the students whenever required. We joined them and had a marvellous week, followed by another week in which I looked after the two small daughters of one of the lecturers. The organisers even hired a hall for Stephan to give a solo recital. It was a most enjoyable break from the very difficult struggle for survival in Paris, where we were constantly hungry.

Shortly afterwards, back in Paris, I met an old Hungarian cellist friend, János Starker. He and two colleagues had been offered a quartet engagement with Radio Hilversum in Holland and were looking for a viola-player to complete the ensemble. When he heard that I was married to Stephan (whom he knew), Jancsi asked if Stephan would consider joining the group. The problem was money. But even this was solved with a loan from the Students' Union and we moved to Cannes where we lived in a hotel. While Starker and his friends had some money, we had very little, but nevertheless managed. Naturally I had to abandon both my studies and my jobs. The plan was for the ensemble to practise for approximately four months and then take up the engagement in Holland. The first violinist, Alfred Indig, an older Hungarian with money and a Dutch wife, was supposed to have secured the

engagement. Unfortunately, his playing was far below the standard of the other three members of the ensemble. The quartet gave
some concerts in Cannes and the surrounding area but it was quite
apparent that the performances were not all that good. By this time
the euphoria passed and the reality of failure had to be faced.

Following this disappointment, Stephan and I returned to Paris
on our beam ends in desperate circumstances. Fortunately the
Students' Union waived our debts but we did not quite know what
to do next. The penury in which we lived was entirely the result of
being uprooted, and our refugee status still stemmed from the
Holocaust.

Stephan thought we should attempt to return to Hungary. I was
very much against this. However, I knew that it would take months
to obtain permission from the Russians and their Hungarian satel-
lites – this was 1947 – and I still hoped that something would turn
up for us. Meanwhile, I took on any work that came my way, even
sewing shirts by piecework, for which I was completely unsuited. I
was always a very exact but slow worker, and sewing shirts
required speed since one was paid by the number of shirts completed. I could hardly manage to finish one shirt in a twelve-hour
day, and usually came home completely exhausted and often in
tears. In addition, I had my singing again and some work at the
Hungarian House. My university course was interrupted, but I felt
that it was already a dead loss. In any case, I could not continue my
main course of study, and the music course seemed both valueless
and uninteresting. I accepted any work that came my way but not
much was available and there seemed no future in the way we were
subsisting – especially with Stephan earning nothing. We were
hungry and had to wear clothes obtained from a charity. I could not
even afford a pair of stockings in the winter.

By this time, we were living in the Latin Quarter at the Hotel
Welcome on the corner of Boulevard St. Germain and the Rue de
Seine. In those days the hotel was very much run down, although
one step up from that in which we had lived in the Jewish quarter.
Several penniless musicians, mainly Hungarians, lived at the Welcome and the environment was congenial. There was a market in
the street (it is still there) where cockles were the cheapest item to
buy, so we lived on cockles and egg-powder and occasionally

horsemeat. We still could not afford anything which was not available on ration and therefore expensive. Whenever something came out on ration (mainly meat), it quickly disappeared from the shops and was only to be got on the black market. We hardly ever went out anywhere, for we simply could not afford any recreation. One day Stephan went to a concert given by the violonist Yehudi Menuhin and called at his dressing-room to request a complimentary ticket. Menuhin gave it to him and, after chatting with him, gave him two tickets for a concert the following night to enable me to attend. Somehow we also obtained a ticket to a concert performance by another celebrated violinist, Jacques Thibaud.

By now we were really desperate and it looked as if we would have to go back to Hungary. Stephan did not mind that much, largely because he had not been in Hungary to experience anti-Semitism as I had. His wealthy father had wisely sent him to Brussels, ostensibly for additional studies but in reality to get him out of Hungary before the war. When Belgium was occupied by the Germans, Stephan fled to France, seeking sanctuary first in Lyons and then in Marseilles. During the latter part of the war he was in hiding in Marseilles, but he had a Hungarian passport in which his religion was falsified and he did not have pronounced Semitic features. In Marseilles, he had even managed to play in the orchestra under the baton of Paul Paray. It was only after the war that he could not get a work permit.

One day Starker told us that he had seen an advertisement for musicians for the symphony orchestra in Durban, South Africa, and suggested Stephan should try for an audition with the orchestra's representative in Paris. I went with Stephan and became friendly with the English interpreter, a charming elderly French lady. I told her how desperate we were for Stephan to obtain work as a viola player with the Durban orchestra. I learned later that Stephan had been considered far too good for the position and that Edward Dunn, the Musical Director of the Durban Civic Orchestra, feared that he would not remain with the organisation. But my plea had helped, and Stephan received a contract to join the orchestra.

However, while waiting, we passed through a very trying time. One day in September 1947 was particularly difficult. I returned to the hotel at the end of my tether. Stephan was in the room of our neighbour, the young Hungarian violinist, Robert Gerle, and was in a dreadful state. He had received the contract from Durban that morning but declared that he could not take up the appointment because he was mad. Robert and I tried to reason with him but he kept repeating that he was mad and incapable of taking any employment. I was at my wits' end. Here we had been struggling fruitlessly for so long and now there was hope for a job and a future and Stephan was refusing to take it. A few days later, he agreed to accept the contract but from then on he began to behave very strangely, displaying the symptoms of – as I later found out – schizophrenia. He also attempted to commit suicide but made sure that he did not succeed.

Meanwhile, I had a stroke of luck. Though I could not type I applied for an advertised job with the American Joint Distribution Committee (JOINT) as a typist and with the assistance of the receptionist, an elderly gentleman who had helped me with the typing test, I got the position. Luckily I did not have to type and was given all kinds of jobs. I was the lowest paid employee, but at least it was a congenial atmosphere and with people who were friendly. At this point I needed all the kindness I could get, for there was no limit to Stephan's bizarre imaginings, which conjured up all sorts of frightening situations. Although I continued to sing in choirs, I earned just about enough to feed one person, and I began to cheat. I would eat nothing all day and in the evening cook for Stephan but eat very little, saying that I had had lunch at work and that the doctor had told me that it was important for Stephan to be well fed. This went on for some time and I was becoming ever more desperate.

Then, one night Stephan thought of a new way of committing suicide. He would kill me, the authorities would execute him and that would solve everything. I woke up in the night as he was throttling me. I managed to get out of his grip but then and there I decided that I had to leave him. I was much too frightened to continue putting up with him.

Helen, a delightful woman who also worked at the JOINT in Paris – she was formerly from Berlin and now South African – took me home with her. After a few days a room became free where she was staying and I moved in. I went back every day after work to do the shopping and cooking and washing and whatever Stephan needed, but returned to sleep in my new quarters. I had a delightful room in a beautiful house owned by an elderly countess, and Helen and her boyfriend were most helpful and supportive. It certainly made life pleasanter but it did not make things easier for me.

A psychiatrist friend who saw Stephan at this time advised me either to get him into a mental hospital or ensure that he got to South Africa to take up the position. He thought that if I opted for the hospital alternative, having no money, Stephan would just rot away and perhaps never be released. Psychiatric hospitals in France, our friend explained, were extremely bad, except for the private ones. On the other hand, the fact that he had work and would be a member of an orchestra might restore his balance of mind. It was a gamble, but he thought I had nothing to lose and much to gain. I therefore decided in favour of South Africa.

But Stephan insisted that he could not go. A priority passage had been booked for him, and when the time came for his departure in November 1947, I had to coax him from the room into the taxi, from the taxi on to the train, and then on to the ferry right until we arrived for embarkation in Southampton. It was a harrowing experience; wherever we stopped Stephan sat down and refused to go any further. Things were further aggravated by the fact that I was constantly hungry, for the extras of the trip (Stephan's passage was paid for but not the expense of my accompanying him to the ship) had taken up the major part of my salary and there was little money left for even the most meagre food. I had also had to pay two rents over the past few weeks. But I had my return ticket to Paris and though it was agreed that I would follow Stephan (in 1947 places on ships were strictly limited) when my passage came through in an estimated six months, I had already decided not to go to South Africa but to seek a divorce. It was not Stephan's illness alone that led me to conclude that our marriage was a mistake. Our ideas about cleanliness, our principles and our aesthetic sensitivities were all completely different. In addition, I found Stephan's constant punning quite unbearable. I felt that I had been driven into the marriage through having lost most of my family and friends owing to the Holocaust, and would never have married him in normal circumstances.

On the day that I put Stephan on to the ship, French seamen joined a general strike and there was no ferry for me to return to Paris. I managed to contact some Hungarian friends who lived in London, and they put me up for a few nights. I was afraid that I would lose my job. While in London, I was offered employment with the Coram Nursery but I had to return to Paris to wait for a British work permit. And I was not even sure that I wanted to leave Paris. Even though I had a hard time there, I had many friends, I always delighted in the beauty of the city and loved the French language.

Six days had passed, and there was still no end to the strike. A childhood friend bought me an air passage to Paris and one November morning I left for the French capital. It was my first flight, due to take an hour and a half. I had no money nor had I a watch. As the plane took off, it was grey all round us. The stewardess asked me if I wanted breakfast, which I declined, not realising I did not have to pay for the meal. We flew through heavy cloud and I could see nothing. The time went very slowly and seemed to be much longer than one and a half hours. When the stewardess offered lunch I was perplexed that two meals should be offered over so short a time. In my pecuniary situation I again refused. We seemed to be flying round in circles. Finally, after five hours in the air we descended and were back in London! Apparently we had done the journey twice over; because of the prevailing fog we could not land in Paris, and we had just enough fuel to get to London. We were told to return in the evening when the airline would try again. But by the evening the fog had thickened and no plane could take off.

While waiting to board the plane, I met three of my colleagues from the JOINT who had come to London for the weekend and were also stranded. Then a man approached us saying that he was also trying to get to Paris and had a friend who owned a private six-seater plane. If we joined him, he could arrange for his friend to take us. We agreed and went to a hotel (my colleagues advanced some money for a room) where we awaited his call. Quite late the next morning, he called us and told us to go to Folkestone, because the plane could not land in London. By the time we got to Folkestone it was too foggy there as well and we had to spend another night in a hotel. On the following day the plane finally arrived and it was agreed that the pilot should take us to Le Touquet where a car would wait for us, as there were no trains. The plane was only a tiny four-seater and the pilot had to make two trips. Although it was a thrill to fly in a small 'glass case' of a plane, it also made me feel vulnerable. On our arrival at Le Touquet there was no car for us. We waited to see what would happen. A few hours later we heard that a train would be leaving in a few minutes. In a mad rush, we managed to board the train which was so overcrowded that it seemed to be bursting at the seams. We got to Paris ten minutes earlier than the conductor had announced and as quickly as we emerged, the train sped out of the station. Within eight minutes of its departure it was blown up by strikers. We were really fortunate that luck was on our side.

On my return from London I was feeling very weak and unwell. A doctor whom I consulted advised me to go to a convalescent home to rest and to be properly fed because I was suffering from malnutrition. I was able to secure admission to a student convalescent home in Combloux in the Haute Savoie, where I stayed for a month. What a glorious time I had there! First of all I met a French girl, Françoise, who became a lifelong friend. An international student congress took place in Combloux over the Christmas holiday which was most invigorating intellectually, and we had some superb food and music. The Végh Quartet rehearsed at our 'Chalet des Etudiants' and I became very friendly with Éva Czakó, the wife of Janzer, the viola player. Éva herself was a superb cellist, whom I had known as a very young pupil of János Starker. During one week, I also enjoyed being allowed to plan and present a gramophone record programme on our internal broadcasting system. There was snow, but we were warm and went for long walks; once again I felt young and confident that I could start life anew. I stayed at Combloux for a month and by mid-January 1948 I was back in Paris working at the JOINT.

I had started working for the organisation while Stephan was still in Paris. At first I was assigned to duties wherever someone with no special foreign language knowledge, except English, was required. I also stood in for the receptionist whenever he left the office, doing simple office jobs. But as my employers became aware that I knew several languages I was soon assigned to press cutting work, scanning the newspapers and extracting anything with a reference to the JOINT. This work provided much insight into the functions of the organisation and much experience in office administration which I had only previously had in the Hungarian House. It also widened my knowledge of world events. I enjoyed working with my colleagues and with the extremely pleasant and intelligent Polish head of our department.

In the office, I became very friendly with a Hungarian woman a little older than I. She was now divorced and lived alone. She came from a humble background, was intelligent, knowledgeable and most keen to learn and read widely. Alice was a lovely warm person and we became very fond of each other.

There was one oddity about her: every time she read about a fictional character she seemed to assume the role for a short while. One day, she was telling me about a book that moved her very much. I do not recall its title but it was the story of a man who had committed suicide. No one could understand why. He had been very successful, seemed happy with his wife and five-year-old son, had a mother to whom he was devoted and whom he often visited. He also had a brother with whom he was on very close terms; he even had a lovely girl-friend. The man had no worries and a well-ordered life. In the book, everyone developed a theory and related what they thought might have been the cause of the man's demise. Even the local policeman, who had the deepest respect for him, had a theory. Yet, nobody really knew why he had taken his life.

Then, one day his little son was sitting on the kerbside with a friend and said that before his father had died he had told him an exciting oriental story about a little mouse. The mouse lived with his family and was very happy except for one thing. Whenever he saw birds flying he too wanted to fly. His wish was granted and suddenly he could fly. He was so happy! He flew among the birds and saw all the wonderful things that birds see high in the sky – the cities, cathedrals, forests and castles. It was marvellous, but it became rather lonely. So the mouse learned the language of the birds in order to be able to converse with them. But even though he could now speak to the birds, he was obviously not really a bird and, unintentionally, the birds made him feel that he was not really one of them. The mouse now became homesick and thought how lovely it would be if he could tell all the other mice of all the wonderful things he had seen. And so he went home and the mice were happy to see him, but he soon felt that he was no longer really one of them. And he felt very sad.

Alice became quite involved with this story, kept telling everyone about it and somehow re-enacting it as if she were principally involved. I became worried about her. Soon there was a long weekend and we arranged to meet on the second day at a picture gallery. Unfortunately, during that period, Stephan was particularly difficult and I hesitated to leave him alone. I was unable to get a message to Alice, mainly because she lived quite a distance from us and had no telephone. To make matters worse, there was a transport strike. I was finally able to get to our meeting-place, which was at walking distance from our hotel, but she was not there and I could not wait very long for her. I had a premonition that something had happened to her, and this seemed to be confirmed when the following day she did not come to the office. About half-way through the morning the telephone rang and I instinctively knew that it was news of Alice. She had opened the gas-tap and was dead. I was very distressed but not surprised. Once again the Holocaust had taken its toll. Alice, a Jewess, born in Hungary, because of persecution, felt unwanted there. She emigrated to Paris, but could not feel at home there either, like the little mouse, even though her French was immaculate. No one seemed to have noticed that something was worrying her.

One day our boss became very excited; his sister was coming to Paris. She had survived Auschwitz and he had not seen her since the war. He was sure I would like her and that we would have much in common. When she came to the office I was shocked – I knew her only too well. She was one of the unpleasant Polish Jewish *Kapos* I had been forced to endure in Auschwitz-Birkenau!

In Birkenau we rarely saw German SS women, because it was not necessary for the authorities to utilize them. The Polish Jewish inmates had been brought to the camp three to four years earlier. Many were only 15 or 16 years old, or even younger, when they were incarcerated. Although most of the girls perished within a short time of their captivity, those who survived were extremely tough. Hard and selfish, they cared only for themselves and thought only of survival. They were quite capable of torturing us and were always ready to carry out the orders of their German masters. They had lost all sense of humanity. But there was also probably an element of envy in their attitude towards us, inasmuch as we were still well-fed when we arrived and had come so much later to the camp. They were so spiteful and vicious that at the end of the war a number of these women were lynched by survivors. I never participated in lynching or retribution, because I never believed that behaving to others as they had behaved to us was justified. Yet I could well understand the anger of my co-inmates. Today I can even understand the behaviour of those Polish girls. Anyone who was able to survive for more than a few months in such awful circumstances must have became brutalized, uncaring and selfish. Only with an extremely strong sense of survival at all costs could anyone have lasted longer than his or her original strength permitted.

Thus it was indeed traumatic to meet one of my former tormentors, all the more so because I was fond of my chief and I did not want to hurt him. Then, too, I was very bad at concealing my feelings. And so I tried to be polite and luckily the sister never again came to the office. I never told him about my experience with her – of what use would it have been to tell him the truth?

I learned much in the office about archival work. Later, I was transferred to become assistant to the main filing clerk of the head office, Mrs Helen Tennenbaum. She was a brusque American whom most people disliked because of her short temper and aggressive and sometimes pointed behaviour. But I got on well with her and we became good friends. She kept the filing system of this vast international organisation in fine order and she taught me a great deal about the care and maintenance of records.

8 • South Africa

The JOINT had two categories of staff: foreign and local employees. The foreign staff were well paid and received a special food parcel every month. Because I was stateless but had a French residence permit, I belonged to the local (French) staff, who were miserably paid, and, even though we really needed food parcels to augment our meagre diet, we were excluded from extra rations. We resented this situation. Moreover, when I first went to Paris from Marseilles, I was entitled to a modest sum of money as an ex-deportee for rehabilitation, but I had refused the money because I felt that, as I was young and free, I could earn my own living and did not want charity. Later, working with the JOINT, when I saw how much of the money was spent on receptions and function expenses instead of rehabilitation, I regretted refusing to take the grant and no longer had any qualms about accepting anything from the organisation.

On my return to Paris after getting Stephan on to the ship, I immediately began divorce proceedings. I had decided not to follow him to South Africa. In spite of my poverty, the meagre official rations and scarce food, I felt that there were many others like me. I had many good friends and I really loved Paris and did not want to leave the city. At the time I suddenly felt rich; with Stephan gone, my earnings could now suffice for myself alone. On the other hand, by 1948 with the JOINT gradually decreasing its activities, it was apparent to me that I had no future in the organisation. Thousands of people were striving to obtain visas to go somewhere – to secure what I had, a visa to immigrate to South Africa. I was urged not to give it up. Indeed, many of my colleagues, American and South African women, heard about my problems and somehow I became a cause to them. They assured me that I did not have to stay in Durban and even promised to arrange a job for me as a teacher in Cape Town in a Jewish nursery school. And they promised that if I found that I disliked South Africa, they would pay for my return journey to France. I must, they insisted, at least try it and see how I fared in South Africa.

I felt free, without ties and decided that I had nothing to lose. I was informed that all the necessary steps for my departure would be made by the JOINT. However, the South African government would only admit me with a valid passport. I had none and so I applied for one at the Hungarian Embassy, only to be told that as I had not returned to Hungary after the war, I had relinquished my nationality. As I was arguing my case, András Havas, secretary to the Ambassador, Count Mihály Károlyi, came into the room. Havas was a prominent old-time Communist, who was soon to return to Hungary only to be executed by the Rakosi regime. When he asked what the problem was and asked my name, I told him that my maiden name was Mosonyi. He immediately enquired if I was any relation to Dr Dezsö Mosonyi, and I told him that he was my father. He remembered my father as an active socialist who had been jailed briefly following the fall of the shortlived Bolshevik regime of Béla Kun in 1919. Havas said he would see what could be done and asked me to return in a few days' time. When I duly returned, I received a Hungarian passport valid for one year and this was accepted by the South African Embassy. I was issued with a temporary residence permit valid for three weeks and was assured that at its expiry it would be exchanged for a residence permit which would also permit me to take employment.

At the JOINT all had become interested in my situation and I became something of a *cause célèbre*. When I left in March 1948, some 50 people came to the railway station to see me off. Just before the train left, I asked the chief of the JOINT's Emigration Department, Mr Pines, what I should do if no one from the JOINT was waiting for me when I arrived in Genoa, the port of embarkation, at midnight. He told me not to worry – if no one met me I should go to the Hotel Bristol. In my naiveté, I did not realise he was joking, since the Bristol was one of the grandest hotels.

I arrived in Genoa with the equivalent of five pounds in my pocket. No one was there to meet me. As I did not know my way about and since it was past midnight I went to the Hotel Bristol, which I was amazed to find was of the first-class variety. But I felt completely irresponsible and I enjoyed spending the night in a decent bed in a sumptuous room.

The following morning I went to the local JOINT office. When I told them where I had spent the night they were taken aback. Just then Mr Pines telephoned from Paris to ask if I had arrived safely and roundly reprimanded them for not having sent someone to meet me at the railway station. Mr Pines also instructed them to take good care of me and to make sure that I embarked on the right ship. After this stern dressing-down by Mr Pines, the Genoa JOINT officials accorded me VIP treatment, much to my amusement. I offered to help in the office and moved into a nice little Italian boarding-house for a few days before my departure.

There were thirteen of us travelling through the auspices of the JOINT on the *SS Toscana* in tourist class. It turned out later that there was one South African person in first-class accommodation who was responsible for all of us. As we were boarding the ship it was discovered that my suitcase was missing. Mr Schwarz, the head of the JOINT's Genoa office, was most perturbed. Very near departure my case was found in another ship and quickly brought over to the *Toscana*, much to his relief. He could now relax as I was really on my way.

The *SS Toscana* was an Italian ship which, before the war, had been a cargo vessel. During the war it was a troop carrier for 400 soldiers; now it had become an emigrant ship carrying 1,200 passengers. It was badly overcrowded. Most of the passengers, in addition to our small group, were English emigrants to South Africa or Italian emigrants to East African countries they had got to know during war service. As foreign languages always fascinated me, I joined a group of Italians and the following day, when the ship arrived in Naples, went ashore with them.

My printed schedule of sailing time provided by the Lloyd Triestino Company stated that the ship would sail from Naples at midnight. My companions were not terribly interesting but very jolly and I enjoyed walking about Naples with them. Somewhere, somehow, in company with a man called Pietro Rambaldo I lost the rest of the group. At about seven in the evening (I had a camera with me but no money and Pietro had spent what he had on him), we decided to return to the ship for a meal and then to come off again for a couple of hours until departure. But – oh horror! – when we came to where the ship was moored we found that it had gone! Apparently the time of departure had been changed to six o'clock. This had been on the ship's notice-board when we disembarked, but none of us had noticed it. This was the first time I had ever travelled in a large (10,000-ton) ship and I did not realise that they could change the printed timetable without warning the passengers. Our passports were on board and, without money, we had to spend the night on a bench in a park. Luckily the weather was mild.

Meanwhile, Pietro had fallen for me and our relationship became one huge joke. I was in no hurry to get to South Africa and was game for any adventure. For his part, Pietro was convinced that most other women in such a situation would have cried or become hysterical but I only laughed. I did not encourage Pietro's advances; although pleasant and kind he was not very intelligent. The next day we went to the Lloyd Triestino offices where we were told that we would have to go to Rome and from there take a plane to Port Said where we could reboard the ship in five days' time. We also went to the Naples office of the firm for which Pietro was going to Kenya to work as a draughtsman. They agreed to pay for his journey to Rome and flight to Port Said and gave him enough money to last until Rome. The company also agreed to accept Pietro's guarantee of my air travel to Port Said, and on we went to Rome. How I enjoyed this unscheduled visit – my first – to the Italian capital!

After two days, Pietro's firm arranged a flight for us to Port Said. This was not an easy task in March 1948; there were few flights and all were fully booked well in advance. But there was a problem: the airline demanded payment in dollars and the company's only foreign currency was in sterling. What to do? Although I had been previously determined not to go to the JOINT office in Rome, I now decided to see them, as I would not have to ask them for money, but only to exchange the sterling for dollars. Pietro was paying for my air passage and I had agreed to reimburse him as soon as I started working in Cape Town. So I went to the Rome office. When I got there I found some 50 people waiting to be seen. As I went up to the reception desk to say that I could not wait because it was a matter of extreme urgency, the receptionist, on hearing my name, said they had been searching for me everywhere. Apparently the person who was travelling first-class from the JOINT had notified the Paris, Genoa, Rome and South Africa offices that I had gone missing. They had been very concerned at my disappearance.

I was taken immediately to the head of the Rome office and as I was speaking to him a telephone call came from Paris asking whether they had any news about me. The Rome office quickly arranged the dollar exchange for Pietro and paid for my airline passage on condition that I reimburse them from South Africa when I was working again. I did not tell them that for the past three days we had had no money to buy food or to pay for a hotel and that we had slept rough on park benches.

Now I needed an Egyptian entry visa and the JOINT could not help. I was instructed to go to the Egyptian Embassy and explain my situation but to conceal the fact that I was Jewish. It was now March 1948, not the best time for a Jewess to arrive without papers in Cairo. But the Egyptian Ambassador was a friendly man; we had a long conversation and for some unknown reason, I even sang a number of French student songs for him. He telephoned to inform the Foreign Ministry in Cairo of our impending arrival and requested that the Egyptian police escort us to Port Said to embark on the *Toscana*. All was now arranged and on the following day we went to board the plane. There were still difficulties: I had no passport (it had been left on the ship) and no entry permit to Italy. How could the Italians permit me to depart officially when I was in their country illegally? When the ship moored in Naples, we had been issued with a pass for the few hours' stay in Italy. And so now they could not let me out of the country. After twice putting me on and taking me off the plane, the Italians finally relented and let me depart. I suppose that they had decided that it was more trouble to keep me than to let me go, and so – good riddance!

On the plane to Cairo I slept like a baby. On arrival, at five o'clock in the morning, the Egyptian police boarded the plane and took me off before anyone else disembarked. They took me with Pietro to their headquarters and told us that they would take us to Port Said to the ship. Then news came that the ship had left Port Said. We were taken to Port Suez and en route I saw the desert and camels for the first time and found the journey most interesting, although it was extremely rough going in the motor transport. Poor Pietro was carsick and miserable throughout the journey while I sang French songs with the Egyptian policeman. After a thorough body search, for they refused to believe that I had no money and no papers and only a camera, they handed us over to the captain of the port. Several times I was asked by the Egyptians if I was Jewish, but – for the first time in my life – I staunchly denied being a Jew. We had long conversations with the port captain for whom I sang more French songs. He was so delighted that he wanted to take me on a tour of Suez. I would have loved to go, but as he only wanted to take me and not Pietro, I suspected his motives.

The Cairo police gave us a superb breakfast on arrival, but in Port Suez we only got coffee. At about 11 pm, the captain had to go on board to inspect the luxury liner *Canberra*, and he took us with him. I enjoyed this but poor Pietro was again seasick and felt completely dejected. Finally, at 2 am, the *Toscana* arrived and we were taken aboard. It turned out that as we had not appeared in Port Said they had assigned our bunks to new passengers and put our things in store. Worse still, they had left my passport at Port Said. All we could do was sleep on the dining-room floor and eat some left-over cold potatoes.

In the tourist class, the food consisted mainly of dried-bean dishes and potatoes. During the entire voyage we ate neither fruit nor fresh vegetables and hardly any meat. We were really quite lucky to have missed part of the journey because the ship had experienced a very stormy crossing before entering the Suez Canal, and its cleanliness, or the lack of it, had deteriorated further during our six-day absence.

By next morning, news got round that we were back and I was fêted. What fun! Everybody wanted to dance with me and I had a splendid time, notwithstanding the poor food and the now-restored accommodation. One day I heard some magnificent singing. It was the Italian barman who had a superb tenor voice. Some of the English passengers formed a choir. Their singing was of high standard and their success inspired the Italians to do likewise. But their choir turned out to be a complete shambles – even though its individual voices were far superior to most of the English choristers.

As we neared the Equator, our cabins became unbearable. We brought our blankets on to the deck and slept head to toe and body to body next to each other, like sardines, every night until we arrived in Durban. The ship, day by day, became ever more filthy and by our last week on board we all had scabies. The *Toscana*, we learned, was forbidden to carry passengers after its next trip because it had become completely uninhabitable following an outbreak of typhus (some twenty cases) on board. Meanwhile, we had made some interesting stops on the journey where we were permitted to disembark. In Mogadishu, the capital of Somaliland, I saw the tallest of black men and beautiful native women; in Mombasa, Kenya, we were taken to a dance, at which women were conspicuous by their absence. We danced the night away on a dance-floor which extended over the sea surrounded by an entrancing landscape. In the morning we saw the bulls being brought in for the bullfight. After Mombasa we had two days of stormy weather, which delayed – as it turned out, luckily for me – our arrival in Durban. We found the harbour very attractive surrounded by hills with lush green vegetation. The ship's purser had requested the Port Said authorities to forward my passport to Durban, but when the ship docked on 7 April at 6 am, it had still not arrived.

At the quay, the family of one of the JOINT South African secretaries, Lucy Hoddes, were awaiting my arrival. Lucy had told them about me and they were all most kind and helpful. Lucy's mother, dear 'Ma', took me under her wing and treated me as a daughter throughout my stay in Durban. I shall never forget her goodness. Also on the quay was Stephan, unshaven, shouting a torrent of erotic obscenities at me in Hungarian. It was a terrible experience for me. Fortunately, apart from me, only a couple of people understood what he was saying and they were appalled at his behaviour. I was not permitted to disembark until my passport arrived, late in the afternoon. Had it not come, I would have been confined to the ship, which was due to depart next morning.

Since my visa was connected with Stephan's employment, I had to meet him and I was told that I would have to remain in Durban until my permanent residence permit arrived in three weeks' time. That was the beginning of April 1948. The week after my arrival, the

Smuts government fell and was replaced by Malan's Nationalist government. As my temporary residence permit expired and was not renewed, I had neither residence nor work permission and was obliged to remain in Durban. And so I was never able to take up the job in Cape Town.

When I left Paris, my divorce proceedings had just begun. Fortunately, as Stephan only had a small room where he was not permitted to have anyone to stay with him, for the time being I was put up in a hotel. Like the nocturnal owl, I prefer to sleep in the morning, and since I had had little sleep on the ship, I eagerly looked forward to a long peaceful rest in a clean bed. Imagine my horror when, at 5 am, there was a knock on my door and someone woke me up with a cup of tea! I could never get accustomed to this habit and took several days before I plucked up enough courage to say that I did not want morning tea, or coffee. It then took a few more days to convince the hotel staff that I was serious and did not wish to be disturbed in the small hours of the morning. I am sure that as a result I was considered quite uncivilised. But most urgent was ridding myself of scabies, and a good doctor's ointment did the trick within a week.

Stephan was in a terrible state when I arrived. As the orchestra was on holiday, he came to see me every day and we were often invited out. South African hospitality was generous. On his arrival, Stephan had been interviewed by a newspaper and he had mentioned that his wife, who had been to Auschwitz, would follow him as soon as it was practicable. I had the distinction of being the first extermination camp survivor in Durban and everyone wanted to hear about my experiences during the Holocaust. In the second week I was invited to address a Jewish women's group. I spoke for a couple of hours and then answered questions. At the end of my talk, one of the women came up to me and said: 'My poor dear girl, I am sure you had a hard time but surely your imagination has run away with you a bit?' Another remarked: 'If you were to dress a bit better you would be quite pretty.' This upset me very much; only much later did I fully comprehend the inability of people to envisage the stark horror of the concentration camps and the brutality inflicted on helpless victims. As for the gratuitous advice to improve my attire, all I possessed till then was cast-off clothing given by the better off. I had no choice but to wear what I had. It was quite a long time before I was able to wear the first dress that I bought.

I was told that on his arrival in Durban Stephan had been deeply depressed and incapable of doing anything for himself except play in the orchestra. The orchestra had employed a very nice young black to look after him, to shave him, dress him and get him to rehearsals and concerts. Once he was performing, he was perfectly all right. Since, on my arrival, the orchestra was on holiday, his valet did not attend to him, hence his unkempt appearance on the quayside. But following my arrival he seemed to improve and within a few days he was behaving quite normally. When the orchestra began performing again, he no longer needed a valet. Stephan was now kind and considerate and obviously pleased that I was there. Because I lacked the necessary papers, I could not move on. I had to make the best of things. Stephan was made so happy by my presence, behaving so decently and responsibly, that we decided to try to live together once again. I am not sure that I can explain – even to myself – why I went back to him, apart from the reasons already mentioned. Though Stephan was good-looking, I was never physically attracted to him. Also he lacked the ability to establish satisfactory relationships with people. I suppose that what motivated me at the time was the fact that I was in a completely strange environment, with no family, no security and no residence or work permit. I really had little alternative. In the circumstances I hoped that this time life with Stephan would work out better than before. The repercussions of the war were still with me! We tried to find somewhere cheap to live, but it was difficult. A musician in the Durban Civic Orchestra earned the same pay as bus-drivers (who were themselves low-paid) and I was not permitted to work.

While I was living with the Vidies in Paris, following my release from the Marseilles prison, I was fascinated by the window display of a small but exclusive restaurant opposite their flat. There was always a very large pineapple displayed in the window – and how I longed to taste it! But I was much too poor even to think of such luxuries. Now, in Durban, I was still very poor, but a pineapple was no longer a luxury. One could buy one for a shilling (about five pence). And so at the first possible opportunity I bought a pine-apple. I savoured its glorious taste for only a few moments – then my mouth was full of painful blisters. It seems that the enzymes which make meat tender when treated with pineapple juice in-flamed the inside of my mouth, and I was in agony.

When I left France, I found that any money in the form of coins had no value whatsoever. After my arrival in Durban, Stephan gave me some money. When I changed the notes into coins, I had absolutely no idea of their value. Having so long been deprived of sweets and chocolates, I found the display at Woolworth's much too tempting. I had discovered a sweet which I could not resist; it was a nut surrounded by marshmallow, the whole covered in chocolate, and in the shape of a rounded pyramid. Every day, I returned and bought and bought and continued to buy my favourite sweets. I was so addicted that I could not even wait to leave the shop before eating them. One day I suddenly realised that I had spent seven pounds in a week on these chocolates and became aware that half-a-crown (12½p) was a lot of money. Worse still, this was the only time that I was not earning anything at all and Stephan was supporting me, except for my lodging costs. As long as I was living on my own, my rent was paid by the JOINT.

There was a great shortage of accommodation in Durban. Even though the city had not been bombed and the nearest it had come to the war was the sight of a Japanese ship miles outside the harbour, during the war no building had taken place and the city had experienced a very large influx of immigrants. Being hard up did not help us in the circumstances. I searched for suitable quarters. Wherever I went I was given a cup of tea. Not being a tea addict, I found it too much of a good thing, but it would not have been polite to refuse such a gesture. However, I was unable to find a suitable room. One day, as I was standing at a bus-stop, intending once more to look at a room which had been advertised, I got into conversation with a woman. When she heard of our plight, she offered to share her flat which was in a most convenient area. I was overjoyed and we moved in. After a short time, Mrs Evans (for that was her name) decided that she could put up a bed for herself in her son's flat, which was in the same building, and we could use her flat. We were infinitely grateful but our happiness was short-lived.

This was a municipal flat and Mrs Evans who, by the way, only charged us the rent she herself had to pay, had no right to sublet her flat. Someone informed the Durban council and we were evicted together with poor kind Mrs Evans. Our plight was all the more poignant because by that time I was in my sixth month of pregnancy and Stephan was having recurrent breakdowns and was in and out of a sanatorium paid for by the Jewish community.

At first, being pregnant made me very happy in spite of our poverty. Everything looked hopeful as Stephan improved rapidly and appeared to be normal. He began giving solo performances and started to receive widespread recognition. The Durban Orchestra was not all that good and he hated its light music concerts, especially those given on the beach. We purchased a cheap and plain kitchen table and four chairs – our first belongings – on easy credit. Unfortunately, this caused me much worry later. It was the first time ever that I had bought anything on credit and since that time, I never have again. Everything seemed to go well and we were quite happy. We made many friends and made plans for the future. We also decided that although there were many things we did not like in South Africa, we could see it through for the next five years. Then we would become South African citizens, with passports which would enable us to go to England. We were really anxious to return to Europe, Stephan mainly because he found the heat in Durban unbearable and I because of the political situation and the provincial atmosphere pervading South Africa. Meanwhile it was not at all a bad life. At least we were not hungry, though we still had to count every penny, especially as I got only occasional work – illegally – such as addressing envelopes for the Zionist Federation and other menial tasks.

Unfortunately, things then took a downward turn. Stephan went on improving until he got so well that he fancied himself a genius, then the Messiah, and finally God Himself, issuing and writing down His commandments. I was in the fifth month of my pregnancy and every day there was some new crisis. Stephan again had to be taken into care. But before his final breakdown he played a rendering of the Beethoven violin concerto, the like of which I had not heard before and have never heard since. I thought I was imagining things but a few years ago a cellist who at the time was playing in the Durban Orchestra confirmed my impression that Stephan's performance had been unforgettable. The day after the concert, he had to be taken – forcibly – to the sanatorium for electric shock and other treatment. Since the sanatorium was very expensive, as soon as he was a little better, he was sent home.

At home, he was often violent and threatened to throw me out into the street in the middle of the night. Another time he opened a bank account with our last three pounds and then with the cheque-book bought some £300 worth of goods in one day! Again, he was hospitalised, because he could not understand what he was doing and became aggressive when told to desist. When, the following day, I went to the shops to return the untouched goods, for there was no money in the bank to cover the cheque and because he was mentally ill, I was told rudely: 'Do you hate him so much that you want us to believe he is not normal? He seemed to us perfectly normal.' I had to exercise all my powers of persuasion to convince them to contact the psychiatrist, who confirmed that Stephan was indeed mentally ill and I was speaking the truth. Sometimes he was at home for a day and sometimes for a week, but invariably he went back to the sanatorium.

Living on charity from the Jewish community since I was not permitted by the government to work, I began to make hats and to bake for special occasions. The cakes and biscuits I baked were made with the best-quality materials and since I dared not charge too much lest I lose my custom, I hardly earned anything. My first two hats were for the big Durban horse race, the July Handicap. It was the highlight of the season and my hats were actually filmed. But again I earned very little. Then I had another idea for earning money – a little money at least – to participate in a recipe competition conducted by *The Natal Mercury*. Very naughtily, I assumed the names of friends and sent in several entries and for many weeks I won all the prizes. Then one day I presented the recipe for a Hungarian cheese mixture which required paprika as an ingredient. There was only one tiny Swiss shop in Durban, hidden in a mews, which had real paprika. Thinking that submitting a recipe without indicating where to get the ingredients was unfair, I provided the address of this modest shop. When, a few weeks later I came to purchase paprika I was told that the shop had had a huge demand because someone had written about it in the newspaper and now they had run out of supplies.

When Stephan was at home he played in the orchestra and got paid as long as he did not become manic. At the time he was diagnosed as schizophrenic. When manic, he might do anything – get up during a performance and take the violin out of the hand of the leader and begin playing solo. Another time, he appeared naked on the stage and started playing.

When I was in my eighth month, I went for my usual physical check-up and was told that I had kidney trouble and that an induced labour had to be risked immediately, even though it might endanger the life of the child. At this point, Stephan was at home but could not quite grasp what was happening. Whenever there was a crisis, he began to practise frantically and no one could interrupt him. Some marvellous friends (the Chiats – still good friends today) came and took me to the hospital where my waters were broken, but the child was far from ready and I was in deep labour for five days and five nights. Finally, on 14 February 1949, a boy was born. While I was in hospital, Stephan ran amok and every now and then turned up at the hospital, even in the middle of the night, and made a scene.

Stephan had wanted a daughter. He had a much younger sister, Agi, whom he had treated as his baby. She was extremely musical and he taught her the violin. He never quite got over having had to leave her. Agi had survived – the only one of his family – but he had not seen her since 1937 and now he wanted a daughter as a substitute for this sister. For some unknown reason I also thought that the child would be a daughter and we had therefore only thought of names for a girl. When our son was born, Stephan could not quite accept that it was a boy, and I had to choose a name. He came to the hospital the morning after the birth, saw a baby boy, said nothing, and then went to the register office where he announced that he had come to register a newborn baby. When they asked him the name of the father, Stephan replied that he did not know. As for the identity of the mother, he said it was his wife. Then, on being asked whether he thought I had sexual relations with other men, he replied that he was convinced that I had not, but since he assumed that he was going to be the father of a girl and I had presented him with a boy, how could he know that he was the father? Anyway, the first name that came to my mind – and I was told I had to name the boy straight away – was Ivan. I had two very dear childhood friends who bore that name and wanted my son to have it also.

9 • A son – and Israel

Even before Ivan's birth I was told by the psychiatrists that if Stephan's state did not improve they wanted to attempt a leucotomy to help him. I could see no improvement, and, after taking advice, I consented to the brain surgery. There seemed to be little to lose. But what I was not told was that the operation was still in its experimental stage and the outcome was uncertain. But we were lucky, for Stephan came out of the operation calmer though not better balanced. All the other patients who had this surgery at that time in the Pietermaritzburg Mental Hospital either died or became human vegetables. Stephan seemed to be the only patient to emerge almost unscathed. During his hospitalisation I lived in Pietermaritzburg with an extremely kind family. But, in spite of the leucotomy, Stephan continued to have his ups and downs and was again in and out of the sanatorium.

It was during this time that we were evicted from Mrs Evans's flat and only with great difficulty was the Jewish community able to find accommodation for me. It was a lovely one-room flat with a glass partition. Some time after Ivan was born, I was again forced to move, this time to a miserable room with shared bathroom and conveniences in the courtyard. It was difficult to nurse a baby with rats in the yard and no running water on the premises. Fortunately, some time afterwards, I was moved back into the nice little flat. The Jewish community were extremely good to me, even though their well-intentioned actions were sometimes hurtful. I would have taken any employment or would have done any job, if only I could have worked and not been regarded as an object of charity. At that time, as far as I knew, I was the only refugee in the Durban community and all the good ladies of the community lavished their attention on me.

105

As I mentioned previously, I had no clothes of my own when I arrived in South Africa. Nor could I then afford to buy any. Word got around quickly that I needed clothing. The next day two cabin-trunks full of old clothes arrived at my flat. In the whole lot there was almost nothing I could wear. The same thing occurred when someone decided that a kitchen table (which we bought on credit and could not pay for) was not good enough for me. It had come from a nice Jewish shop, and when I told them that I had to return it, they arranged to defray the cost for me. Suddenly, an enormous Victorian table arrived which hardly left me space to get round the room. Then word got around that I had no money for food and after festivities at the local Jewish club, boxfuls of last night's left-over dry sandwiches were delivered together with large bags full of boiled potatoes. Though I appreciated their intention, thoughtless gifts of this nature made me weep. 'Crumbs which fall from the rich man's table.'

One day I had to go to town. Near the town hall I met a non-Jewish lady I knew. She seemed pleased to see me and invited me to join her for a cup of tea. It was about midday, not quite the time for tea. We went to the nearest hotel lounge. She whispered something to the waiter but he said he was sorry that he could not oblige. I did not know what it was all about. Then we went into a tea-room and she ordered something at the counter. We had a long chat, until the waiter arrived with two double portions of toasted-cheese sandwiches. As soon as they came, she got up and said: 'My dear, I ordered these for you. You must be very hungry, I must run now.' And off she went. I dissolved into tears and could not touch any of the food; it was hurtful in the extreme to be treated like a pauper, however well-intentioned the woman might have been.

But dear Lil Cohen was a very different person. She often invited me to her home and treated me as a friend, not as an object of charity. One day she took me to a dress-shop and let me choose a frock which she bought for me. It was a pretty light-brown maternity dress with white spots and was the first dress I ever wore which I had chosen myself. This was in December 1948, and not until the end of 1951 did I next choose a dress for myself; on that occasion at last I paid for it out of my own earnings.

It reminded me of a time in 1944 when, working in Budapest and earning very little, I went home for Christmas. My father who up till then had kept me on an incredibly tight budget, decided that as my twentieth birthday was approaching, he would dress me from head to toe as a birthday gift. I spent most of the Christmas holiday choosing materials, discussing styles with a first-class dressmaker and getting myself measured for shoes. I was anything but vain but I was very excited about having a completely new outfit.

As I was the only girl in my mother's family, all their spare women's clothes were usually sent to us and then altered into admittedly very pretty dresses, but they were not my choice. I never had a dress which I had personally chosen or which was new. We had a very good dressmaker who came once a month, and another woman looked after the underwear and linen once every three months. The dressmaker, Ilonka, had come to our home as a sempstress at the tender age of 16. She was cheerful, intelligent and friendly, and I had known her for as long as I could remember. I adored her and always looked forward to her arrival. My mother recommended Ilonka to all of her friends and she had established a regular connection. Ilonka was considered to be almost one of our family and when she married it was my parents who gave her away. When she had a son it was my father who brought the child into the world. Ilonka was very clever with her hands, had good taste and had good ideas for making old things look new and pretty. Later, when Hungary was occupied by the Germans, we gave Ilonka a few family heirlooms to keep for us in the event that we might return from deportation. But when after the war my brother returned and asked for the items in her possession, Ilonka denied ever having received them.

We always wore hand-made shoes, not only for health reasons, but also because one of my father's patients, whose wife produced a child almost annually, paid her medical bills by making shoes for the entire family. Thus twice a year we went for our measurements to good old Mr Hidvégi. I can still recall the smell of his workshop. My footwear was always practical, mainly lace-up boots. This time, for my twentieth birthday, I was to have some real ladies' shoes made for me in various colours – though mainly blue because that was my favourite colour. All these wonderful gifts were to be ready for my birthday in April 1944 . . . However, before that day, Hungary had been occupied by the Germans, and my father had been arrested and taken away. It was no time for new clothes.

Ivan was born weighing only two and a half pounds, but he was quite healthy. I tried to breast-feed him but had to abandon my attempts by the fifth day. My milk was not good for him; it made the child increasingly restless. On the very day of Ivan's birth, Stephan again had to be taken into care and I did not know what was going to happen. I had a child but no residence or work permit and a husband in and out of care. I was also worried that Stephan might do the baby harm and therefore, soon afterwards, I agreed to have him certified. He was taken to the mental hospital in Pietermaritzburg, where I visited him once a week.

While I was looking for work, still illegally, and during my weekly visits to Stephan, a lovely 16-year-old Zulu girl came occasionally to look after Ivan for a few hours. She was very bright, smiling, with great charm and sweetness and her English was impeccable. She had been well educated at a missionary school and her father and both her brothers were white-collar workers. It was a pleasure to have her around and she seemed to love Ivan. By this time he was three months old and had just begun to smile, which he now did continually.

One day I left Ivan with the girl, but had to return unexpectedly, since I had forgotten something. I was flabbergasted at what I saw. This girl, with the mind of a educated European woman, was standing half-naked with the child in her arms and a pair of scissors in her hand. She was in a trance and did not even notice my return; she was cutting snippets of her hair and letting them fall on the child's body. I dismissed her instantly. Later I learned that this ritual was a tribal way of demonstrating her affection for the child. Quite possibly I was wrong to dismiss her, but her primitive behaviour frightened me.

Meanwhile, I was growing more and more depressed. The doctors had informed me in writing that there was no hope for Stephan's complete recovery. But every time his condition improved slightly they would send him home to me. When I asked the physicians whether they thought it would make much difference to Stephan if I left with the child, they told me that, in view of my depressed state, it was best that I leave him. They feared that the pressures were becoming too much for me. I had had no real break since my release from concentration camp. And so I decided to ask the Jewish community to help me one last time – in fact it was really the very first time I had asked for assistance, everything else had been offered to me without my asking. I requested funds to pay for the emigration of Ivan and myself to Israel where I hoped I might begin a new life. The community responded in a very generous way and an entire container was filled with suitable furniture to take with us.

After his very difficult first few months Ivan had caught up fast and was now six months old, a big and beautiful baby, always smiling, good-tempered and all in all a great pleasure and solace for me. This was even more astonishing since when he was born he was covered with hair and was frighteningly ugly. Having been trained as a nursery nurse, I did not have the usual first-baby difficulties or fears for I knew what to do and had very definite ideas about child upbringing. In his fourth month Ivan took on human shape and it was obvious that he was a lovely child. The day after I came home from hospital, a woman came to my door and told me she was Dr Sophie Jackson, a paediatrician and general practitioner who wanted to see the new baby. She requested that I come to her surgery once a week and call on her whenever I thought something was wrong. One day, when Ivan was in his fourth month, I went to the surgery. One of the other mothers, remarking what a beautiful baby Ivan had become, reminded me that she and others had been really worried on my behalf when ugly little Ivan was born! Sophie Jackson (later Beecham) was an immense help and support and has always remained a good friend.

As I was trying to earn some money – still illegally – I went to a milliner to see whether I could get some work which I could do at home. The proprietor was not there but a pleasant young girl, Nina, listened to me and then said she might have an idea. She asked if she could come to see me at home. Nina came and told me that she wanted to do private millinery work and could employ me if she could use my flat as her headquarters. This seemed an excellent suggestion for our mutual benefit and we worked out a plan of campaign. For the next few months Nina came every day and I also earned some money. Now I was able to get out, deal with other matters or visit Stephan without having to worry about what to do with Ivan. It seemed an ideal solution, and we became close friends.

One day I was offered a ticket to a recital by the pianist, Julius Katchen. It was a Jewish charity concert and Durban Jews were generally not very interested in serious music. Katchen must have sensed the indifference and he responded with a flamboyant performance. The slow movement of Beethoven's Appassionata was taken at a snail's pace, and the fast movement was much too showy. As an encore, he played some Brahms Hungarian dances in a manner which was not much to my taste. I was quite upset, for having listened to his records and hearing him on the radio, I knew that he was an outstanding musician. After the concert, I was introduced to him by someone who remarked that as I was Hungarian, I must have loved his playing Hungarian music. I fear that I bluntly told him of my disappointment with his performance and declared that a good musician should not play down to his audience. We had a long discussion. Katchen was charming, and took my criticism in good part. Many years later, in London, I heard him again. As he was then playing with Starker, I went into the artists' room after the concert. I thanked Katchen for his exhilarating performance and I reminded him that we had met years ago in Durban. He looked at me and straight away recalled our conversation of some 25 years earlier without my prompting him. He told me that he had thought I was absolutely right and that he never again played down to the public. He was a superb artist and I greatly admired him. By that time Katchen was very ill and he died a few months later.

One day Nina had some guests, two men from Johannesburg who asked her out to a night-club. She invited me to join them. We found a baby-sitter and I was really looking forward to going out for a relaxing evening. As it turned out, it was very dull indeed. A night-club in Durban in those days meant dimmed lights, a not-very-good dinner – we had to bring our own drinks – and some dancing. The men were utterly boring and we did not stay long. The following day, two women members of the Jewish community came to tell me they had heard that I had been to a night-club and did not think it proper for me to do so. I resented this strongly as it seemed that in return for the help I had received from the Community, I must account for all my actions. I had only accepted the minimum of communal assistance and all I had asked for was help to get work – any work – to enable me to earn my living. I could not tolerate being owned by my benefactors. This made me even more determined to leave South Africa and I redoubled my efforts to emigrate to Israel. It would be a long-forgotten dream come true.

Ivan had been born on 14 February (St Valentine's day) 1949. We left for Israel exactly six months later on 14 August. In Johannesburg, some friends were kind and helpful, and from there we boarded a plane, a Dakota, for Israel. Ivan was the only child aboard and, as he was nearly always smiling when not sleeping, he won the heart of our fellow-passengers. We flew very low over what was then Rhodesia and saw blackened landscape with burnt-off stubble. We stopped first at Ndola and, very soon after take-off, had to make a forced landing in a forest clearing. It was well controlled and no-one was injured. We were taken to Lusaka (the Zambian capital), where we spent the night until the plane was repaired. Our next stop was at Entebbe, in Uganda. But before that we flew extremely low and I tremendously enjoyed the exciting sights, herds of buffalo, elephants, zebras and giraffes, all clearly visible. Then we saw the Victoria Falls and the beautiful Lake Victoria. We stopped at Entebbe for a few hours. We spent the night in Khartoum and then next day went on to Wadi Halfa, also in the Sudan, where the heat was so intense that when we got out of the plane I fainted. I still remember how it felt, as if someone or something had hit me on the nape of the neck. Meanwhile, Ivan was smiling all the time in his basket, which was only a washing basket. Then, at last, we arrived at Lydda and we were in Israel!

It was a very exciting moment. My cousin Gucki, who was then living in Holon with his wife and a son, came to meet me. It was wonderful to see him again. I was put up at a hotel for the first night by the Zionist Organisation's South African branch, who were very helpful. The next day I went to see a distant relative, Anita Cohen-Mueller. She was originally from Vienna and, as the first woman Zionist to emigrate from Austria, was a well-known personality of

111

the Zionist old guard. At first she was rather off-hand but soon softened, plying me with advice and giving me a letter to Sister Rosa, the head of the WIZO baby home in Jerusalem. It was thought best for me to put Ivan there for a short time until I could find proper accommodation and get settled. Aunt Anita thought that Ivan should be given a Hebrew name and proposed that I call him Ilan – the poetic expression for a tree. I thought it a beautiful name and promptly accepted her suggestion. A few years later I came across a 1949 calendar where I found that the day on which Ilan was born was Hag Ha-Ilanot, the New Year of the Trees, which is also known as Tu Bi-shvat (the 15th day of the Hebrew month of Shvat) and is celebrated in Israel by the planting of saplings. The name, therefore, was even more appropriate. Aunt Anita also gave me a letter of introduction to the Beth Ha-Halutsot, a Jerusalem women's hostel. The next day I went to Jerusalem. At first I stayed briefly at a not very clean hotel where I was mercilessly bitten by lice, with dire consequences.

Sadly I deposited Ilan at the WIZO baby home and was told by Sister Rosa that I was welcome to see him every day. This was a consolation, for the separation very upset me very much. I hoped that it would not be long before we were together again. Anyway, I had no choice, and I had to consider myself lucky, for it was not easy to get a place for a child at the home. At the Beth Ha-Halutsot hostel I shared a room with three young women – a pleasant American girl and two Bulgarian medical students, with a lamentable knowledge of hygiene. We had considerable difficulty with them for that reason. It was a pity, for they were really very nice girls. They never even took off their underwear to wash themselves or to sleep and, since we arranged to take turns at cleaning the room, the Bulgarians were a problem.

Meanwhile, I had a little luck: nursery school teachers were in short supply, but to work at a nursery school I needed to learn Hebrew as quickly as possible. Fortunately for me an enterprising Russian Jewish Hebrew teacher, Dr Mordechai Kamerat, had persuaded the education authorities to try out one of his ideas, a new method for learning Hebrew rapidly. Thus the first Ulpan (intensive Hebrew course), the Etsion in Bak'a, Jerusalem, came into being. The idea was that people who had a useful profession but could not practise it without knowing Hebrew should be offered the opportunity to study the language intensively. I was accepted for the first trial period of the course one week after it had started. As I knew the Hebrew alphabet and a few words, I began in the second class. When, on the first day, I was told to translate a short newspaper article by the next day and, after hours of struggle, could not quite do it, I started to cry. A Yugoslav international lawyer, Kornel Lorand, whom I sat next to, scolded me and angered me by remarking that just because someone was pretty it did not entitle them to take part in the course. As a result, just to show him, I pulled myself together and made a special effort to complete the assignment. Lorand and I were soon competing with each other and quickly became good friends. Later he admitted that he had been rude with this intention in mind. His ruse really got me going with my studies.

Today the Ulpan is a well-established feature of Israeli life. Anyone who can pay can attend one; there are numerous residential and non-residential courses. But the course at Bak'a was the first of its kind. It was 1949, four years after the end of the war, and here I was still trying to find my feet in the world.

The Ulpan was housed in a large old Arab building, which during Israel's War of Independence suffered damage in a bombardment. There were 70 of us on the course, usually four to a room, and at the beginning we all had to share the only unbroken wash-basin. It was September 1949 and the effects of the War of Liberation still lingered. It was Spartan living. We each had an iron bed and a nail or two on which to hang our clothes. The food was adequate, mainly consisting of different variations of aubergine and fish-fillet, the latter not quite what we understand by fillet today. The fish came in slabs in large boxes from Scandinavia and portions were chopped off for preparation in various ways, mainly fried. We had halvah and olives and an ample supply of bread, but that was about all. No meat, green vegetables, salads, or oranges – the citrus fruit cultivated went for export. I had no money to supplement my diet but that did not really worry me; I never went hungry. We had four hours of tuition every morning and after lunch, four hours of supervised homework. Usually, I then went to the baby home to visit Ilan. It took about half an hour to get there and often Lorand

and Ora, a French friend I had met at the Ulpan, would come with me. Then back to study until midnight. The daily average for me was 12–14 hours of study.

By the third week I was feeling extremely unwell. The Ulpan had organised an outing to the historic fortress site of Massada, where I collapsed and was taken to hospital. The lice that had bitten me during that first night in Jerusalem had given me spotted fever, a form of typhus. I was in hospital for one month, sometimes hovering between life and death. As soon as I began to improve, Lorand brought the Ulpan homework and his notes and I managed to keep up with the class. One thing that saved me during my illness was the fact that I always ate well, even when I had an extremely high temperature. (I still have a good appetite and am constantly hungry.) When I was released from hospital I had only another one and a half months more to spend at the Ulpan. Then I was informed that a nursery-school teacher was needed at the Talpioth immigrants' camp and I was sent there to work. I still lived at the Ulpan for the scheduled five months and continued to study during the evenings.

Meanwhile, I visited Ilan almost every day. It hurt me to see him in his bed – the children were rarely brought down to the garden into the fresh air. He seemed to have a calcium deficiency, for the wall behind his bed had a hole that grew larger and larger as he scraped the chalk off the wall and swallowed it. He was very fat and always fretted and cried when hungry or near feeding time. The nurses were very fond of him, for he was invariably cheerful and slept soundly, but they always fed him first in view of the fuss he made if anyone was fed before him. As luck would have it, Jerusalem at that time suffered a polio epidemic and visits to the home were banned. Ilan was on the third floor and all I could do was to stand in the garden, wait until he was brought out on to the balcony and then wave to him. It was wretched not to be permitted to go near him. Then a measles epidemic broke out at the home and Ilan contracted a mild form of the complaint. This was followed by a chicken-pox epidemic to which Ilan also fell victim, again in a mild form. This went on for about six months, during which period I called at the baby home every day but was not allowed near my child.

By that time I was again living in the Beth Ha-Halutsot which was

114

very near the children's home. Two nurses at the home lived in the next room in the hostel. One day I telephoned the home for news of Ilan and, as usual, was told that he was fine. The nurses next door were not supposed to tell me anything, but, following my telephone call, I happened to meet one of them and she told me in strict confidence that I must get Ilan to a hospital because he was very ill. I dashed off to the home, burst in, despite the protests of the kind old Yemeni watchman, and ran up to where Ilan was kept. He was extremely thin and pale, with flushed cheeks and wide eyes, and was obviously very ill. He was in the arms of a nurse. When he saw me he greeted me with a big smile and opened his arms. But then he let out a loud scream, started crying and pushed me away. He had meningitis. I was extremely angry and upset and made a scene, forcing the home immediately to take the child to hospital. There I was permitted to visit him every day, but he did not wish to see me. He would not even let me near his bed and as soon as he saw me entering the ward, he started to scream. It was two months before he allowed me to take him in my arms. I felt that he had a grudge against me for having deserted him – first while I was ill and later because of the ban on entering the home. It was beyond my control and I felt extremely bitter at Ilan's rejection of me. At a most critical period in the child's development there had been an enforced rift in our relationship and all because we had become separated from each other, still as a consequence of my deportation.

I still did not see how I could take him home with me, so I agreed that after recovery he should return to the WIZO home, even though I now had some hope of securing my own accommodation. Fortunately, the meningitis did not leave any noticeable adverse effects on Ilan.

When I had to move out from the Ulpan, I continued to work in the camp nursery, but as my qualifications were not accepted by my employers, my pay was incredibly small. I also had to begin paying for my Ulpan accommodation, and although this was a small sum, for me it was a fortune. I continued to attend evening classes and to pursue my studies in Hebrew and biblical knowledge with Dr Kamerat. These lessons were free and I enjoyed them very much; they also enabled me to pass a government examination to get a job in the Ministry of Finance as a filing clerk. It was an extremely low-paid job, but better paid than at the nursery. On Dr Kamerat's recommendation, I also applied – and after an interview with Dr Martin Buber and other teachers was accepted – for a teachers' training course. I was offered a grant for study. However, as I was now salaried I had to pay for Ilan's keep in the home every month and I could not obtain a grant for his maintenance. I would have loved to participate in the teachers' training course, but it was not to be. And so I took the job at the Ministry of Finance, which also provided me with the opportunity to apply for my own rented accommodation in place of the room I now again shared with the three other girls.

Eventually I was allotted my own accommodation. It consisted of two of the four solitary confinement cells formerly attached to the British military prison, which was now converted into a mental hospital, in Talbieh, a district of Jerusalem. There were four cells and a shower-room with a lavatory, but there was no water or electricity. The two other cells were occupied by Jean David, a Romanian immigrant who later became a well-known painter. He lived there with his Bulgarian girl-friend. We shared the bathroom and lavatory. As time went on, we had water and electricity laid on and painted the little house, which stood in the garden of a former Arab dwelling called Beth Jamal (The House of Jamal). There were barred windows and heavy iron doors which we painted green. There were also scorpions which I used to kill by holding the paraffin-lamp cylinder underneath them, hoping that they would fall into the flame and not on to my hand.

In spite of the many difficulties I had had in establishing myself in the new land, I felt extremely happy in Israel. Somehow, for the first time in my life I felt that I belonged and that I had a home. I loved Jerusalem; it was a most attractive city. But one was often aware of danger when walking outside the wall of the Old City (at the time we could not go inside because it was occupied by Jordan). From the top of the walls Arab snipers occasionally took pot-shots at passers-by. Still, I knew that this was the country in which I wanted to live. There were many things I did not approve of in Israel and at the time I arrived we were not pampered as were later waves of immigrants. Most people had to struggle to get on with life, but there was hope, and slowly each of us found a way to make a living. One could say what one thought and, oddly enough, it was the first place where no one asked why I did not go to synagogue. I felt free. Every time I travelled from Jerusalem to Tel Aviv, I saw new roads and buildings and where there had been stony ground trees were now growing. I felt alive and part of something great. Naturally there were the usual human squabbles and gossip, but it did not matter. This was where I felt I wanted to stay.

According to Jewish law, a woman can ask for a divorce only in very rare cases. Among the mental illnesses which the law acknowledges as a cause for divorce is schizophrenia. I had a letter from the doctors stating that Stephan was an incurable schizophrenic and so I initiated divorce proceedings. My life was finally getting straight again.

In the meantime I had made many friends and had begun to live a nearly normal life, hoping that soon one day I could have Ilan with me again and perhaps meet someone I would like to marry. I met a number of men and even had some marriage proposals, but found none of my suitors acceptable. Unfortunately I seemed to attract emotionally unstable men who attached themselves to me because they thought me strong. It was all rather frightening. For example, there was a Hungarian, whom I met on the day he got his divorce and we became friends. I found him pleasant as a friend but I was not at all interested in him as a man. He began to press me to promise him that as soon as I had my divorce I would marry him. I told him quite plainly that it was out of the question and I asked him not to spoil our friendship, but he continued to bother me and threatened suicide if I continued to spurn him. This emotional blackmail was more than I could stand and we had a row. That very night he did commit suicide. I was very sad, but had no feelings of guilt.

Then I fell in love with a married man whom I had known since my childhood and who – it turned out – had loved me even in those days. Until this time, I had always made it a rule never to become involved with a married man. I had always been very fond of him but had never thought of him as a lover. And then, suddenly, I fell in love. I knew that his marriage was not very happy; his wife, a rather aggressive woman, was most kind to me, however, and I felt somewhat ashamed of my feelings for her husband. We were very much in love, but I did not want to come between them.

All this time I had had no news about Stephan but a visitor from South Africa informed me that he had suddenly recovered a few months earlier. He was out of hospital, playing again in the orchestra and coping very well. I was informed that he was extremely unhappy that Ilan and I were not with him, but too proud to ask for us to return to South Africa. He made no attempt to get in touch with me nor did he offer to help me to support his child – a thought that had occurred to me only much later. My informant thought I should return and join Stephan.

Meanwhile something interesting happened at the office. Having very little work to do in my job and feeling bored, I looked through the rooms and found a number of cases in one of them. Nobody knew what they were or whence they came. I began to sort out the contents of the cases, appropriated a shelf and some boxes and started to classify the material into a system of my own making, utilising the knowledge I had acquired working in the main filing system of the Joint Distribution Committee. When I had classified all the material, I showed it to my boss. These documents, which were from the period of the British Mandate, were of some importance and were thought to have been lost. My employers were very pleased with my efforts and sent me to other departments to help to index more archives.

But I was still on the lowest salary scale and I really needed more money to enable me to bring Ilan home and pay someone to look after him while I earned our living. I was very hard-working but I had one great failing – I had difficulty getting up early and was very slow-starting in the morning. Every day I was late for work but managed to cover my tracks by arranging with a colleague who had the attendance book I was to sign to withhold it pending my late arrival. It was wrong, I know, but I usually stayed longer hours at work and gave more time than required to make up for my late arrival.

I had a small transistor radio which I used to listen to in the morning. Whenever I heard the signature tune for the Arabic broadcast, I knew that I was late. I had to run up the hill to catch my bus. The bus driver knew me and always waited for me. Invariably he started as I had one foot on the running-board. A gentleman always sat next to the door of the bus and every day I fell into his lap as the vehicle jerked forward. I would apologise and he would smile as I sat down. We never spoke. Imagine my astonishment when after many weeks I was allowed to see my head of department to ask for a salary increase and found he was the same man on whose lap I landed every morning. I got the rise. By this time, I was almost in the position of being able to bring Ilan home. My emotional attachment had no future, mainly because I did not want to break up a marriage.

In the meantime – when I no longer needed or desired it – my residence and permit to work in South Africa reached me at the beginning of 1951. I was, however, still stateless. And so I decided to ask for six months' unpaid leave, let my flat for this period and return to Durban to see Stephan. Letting the flat provided me with the money for the journey. I felt that as Stephan was the child's father, I was obliged to give him the chance at least to see Ilan. It was also a useful opportunity to break off my unsatisfactory attachment.

10 • Return to South Africa

I let the flat very cheaply to Miki, a childhood friend, though a generation older than myself, who had been in the Hashomer Hatzair movement in Szombathely. Miki was a charming person, or so I thought. He was married and had two daughters. He complained that he could not get any accommodation and it would help him to use my 'flat'. I let him have it for the six months very cheaply, just to cover my expenses for the trip to South Africa. I felt that he was a member of my old group whom I could trust.

As I had some furniture and other belongings, I asked my best friend Mia to look after them if Miki moved out earlier than planned, which he thought he might do. A few weeks later, Mia visited my flat and reported to me, very upset, that Miki's children had broken my chairs and messed up my other furniture, even though Miki himself had never moved in. Nor did he reply to my letters. Indeed, he sold my flat for quite a lot of money and so I had no place to return to. I cursed him for what he had done. Though I think it highly unlikely that my curses had anything to do with his demise, he died the same year from a heart attack. As a result of his actions I could not return to Israel unless I was willing to start from scratch. It would again have meant my not being able to keep Ilan with me, since I would have had to go and live in another hostel. I just could not face this.

All this was in the future. My last night in Israel was the eve of Independence Day in May 1951, and I danced throughout the night in the streets and squares and drowned my sorrow at having to leave Israel – even if only for a short while as I then thought. At the same time I was elated to be taking Ilan out of the home at last and, after almost two years, we were again united.

The next morning friends accompanied me and witnessed my joy

120

at taking Ilan with me. He was just over two years old and spoke only a few words of Hebrew – the nurses did not have much time to speak to the children. He was very excited to see the cars in the street and was laughing and pointing at them. It was quite wonderful to see him so happy. But I was sad to board the plane that same afternoon. The flight to South Africa was quite uneventful and Stephan was at Johannesburg to meet us. We travelled back together to Durban. The accommodation we now found was a basement flat, which turned out to be rat-infested! Soon after my arrival I had to have a varicose vein operation and was terrified by the rats in the flat while I was convalescing.

Luckily, before long we moved into another flat which we were to occupy for almost all of the next six years. I found employment as a teacher in the local Jewish nursery school and was in charge of all the Jewish activities. Ilan came with me and caught up very fast, learning English, but still understanding Hebrew, which I tried to keep up for him. Being a friendly, quiet and bright little boy, he became very popular.

Stephan was happy in the orchestra, often performing as soloist. He also gave radio and chamber-music recitals and travelled to Johannesburg and other towns to give solo violin and viola performances. But I was homesick for Israel and though outwardly we remained together, we lived separate lives. I participated in his music-making by listening and criticising and began to play the cello again in the local amateur orchestra and with chamber groups.

One day the teacher in the infant school became ill and the headmaster asked me first to help out, and later, when she decided not to return, to take her place. I also taught Hebrew and religion to older children who attended non-Jewish schools in the morning, and had several private pupils. I was put in charge of a a more advanced class every year. At one point I prepared two pupils for the matriculation examination certificate in Hebrew. I was reluctant to accept them for I had not completed my matric, but the headmaster, Mr Sam Ernst, a remarkable man whom I respected highly, urged me to accept them and to take my own matric examination concurrently. He offered to help me. I was always completely useless at examinations. My two pupils finished with honours, whereas I, who taught them all they knew and prepared them for their examination, barely managed to get through! Invariably, my mind went blank during examinations, and by the time I understood what I had to write I never had time to answer all the questions. However, what I wrote was good enough so that I always managed to scrape through.

At this time, we kept open house for our many friends, for whom I enjoyed preparing meals. Stephan became the leader of the orchestra. Whenever an artist came to the town, we would invite him for a meal or I would prepare a party in his or her honour. Thus I met and was host to the cellists Pierre Fournier and Gaspar Cassadó; the pianist, Louis Kentner; and many Italian opera singers and conductors. I met Andrés Segovia, the guitarist, Claudio Arrau, the Chilean pianist, and many other celebrities. It was a most interesting life, but I yearned for Israel. If not Israel, then I wanted to go back to Europe. To go to Israel with Stephan was a difficult proposition: at that time the only orchestra which would have been suitable for him was the one in Tel-Aviv. But Tel-Aviv had the same humid climate as Durban and in Durban every summer affected his health; he could not stand the heat and was always very near a breakdown. This was something I had already considered before returning to South Africa, for otherwise I would have asked him to come to Israel when we were there.

There were also some problems with Ilan. In the beginning he was always eating, as if to make up for what he had lacked in Israel. Twice he was so ill that he had to be hospitalized, but the diagnosis was always overeating. Most of the time, however, it was possible to reason with him and he understood that he had to stop eating so much. When he was about three, he developed sugar in the urine. In South Africa, children consumed vast quantities of sweets and ice-cream and drank Coca Cola and other sweet drinks. Ilan was constantly invited to play with other children but refused the sweets he was offered. He took his own diabetic sweets and raw vegetables on which to nibble wherever he went. The parents of the other children were amazed at this discipline by one so young.

Ilan never picked a fight and even aggressive children were restrained from fighting when he was their playmate. He was popular with the mothers and the nannies because they knew that if Ilan was present they did not have to worry. He was extremely inventive and the other children were never bored or naughty in his company. It was a great relief for me. I worked long hours in two schools twenty miles distant from each other and I knew that someone was always willing and happy to have Ilan for the afternoon.

We had employed a charming young Zulu boy, Leonard, aged 15, to help me in the home and with Ilan. He was a well-mannered, presentable lad, who spoke no English when he came to us, but was extremely obliging with a happy disposition. We became very fond of him and regarded him as one of the family. As I spoke to Ilan in Hebrew, Leonard began to pick up words and sentences, and only later realised that it was not English. When he came to us he could not boil an egg but enjoyed watching me cooking. One day I came home later than usual and had not prepared the meal; Leonard surprised us by having a perfect meal ready for us. From then on I often let him cook and taught him to prepare many dishes. He could not write and he noted down the recipes by drawing the ingredients, such as two eggs and a heap to represent flour.

As time passed I stopped working in the nursery school and in the mornings began to work at the infant school which was upstairs in the same building as the nursery. Ilan was four when one day he asked his teacher's permission to read to the children at story-time. The teacher gave him the book and Ilan read a story word-perfect. Since it was one that the group had read before, the teacher thought he had somehow memorised it. As she questioned his ability, Ilan firmly insisted that he had read the tale. To test him, the teacher gave him a book which they had never read before and Ilan proceeded to read that fluently, too. On the following day, he said he wanted to count. He counted to 150 and added and subtracted some complicated sums. The teachers were very impressed, especially on the third day, when he came to the nursery school and told the teacher that he wanted to go upstairs to the infant school. When he was told that that was not possible, he threw a terrible tantrum. The teachers did not know what to do with him. Finally they spoke to the headmaster, who decided that Ilan should be granted his request, thinking that he would get bored and want to return to his nursery group.

The starting school age was five and the school year had begun in

January. Ilan had turned four in February and it was now the beginning of April. He joined my Hebrew class. As the children had only just begun to learn to read English, I took the Hebrew reading extremely slowly. I used an attractive but very expensive book of which we had just the exact number of required copies and not one over. We never let the children take these books home and always locked them up after lessons. When I counted the books at the end of the lesson, I found one missing. I looked high and low but it was nowhere to be found.

At home I maintained one very strict rule. As I worked very hard and was extremely busy during the day, I insisted that the hour between six and seven should be for Ilan. He went to bed at six, and then I sat with him and we read or talked or played, whatever he wanted to do. That evening hour was sacred to me and no one could disturb it. Three days after Ilan joined the infant school class, he asked at his bedtime that we read Hebrew that night. I agreed but I had not brought a Hebrew book home with me. At this point he told me that he had the book which had disappeared and that he would read it to me! There were 60 lessons in the book and a vocabulary – which I had not mentioned to the children. In class, we were on lesson five, but in the three days Ilan, who had discovered the vocabulary, had learned it completely and could read all of the 60 lessons fluently.

This quite frightened me. Ilan being so advanced presented a problem at school. He demanded special attention because he was so good, but by virtue of that, he was the one who did not need it. So I made him my assistant and he proved most adept at teaching slow learners, showing infinite patience with his classmates. He got on equally well with the other class-teacher and so he remained at the infant school. Within four weeks Ilan was at the top of the class. I never found out how he had learned to read and count.

Our Zulu boy, Leonard, tried to keep up with Ilan, who taught him to read and write. They were very fond of each other and had great fun together. Stephan and I were also very fond of Leonard. As we were against the exploitation of blacks, we paid him more than most people would have done and he seemed happy with us. Leonard did my shopping and I made arrangements with the local grocery shop for him to purchase the items we needed daily – I made a list. The grocer recorded in a book the price of what had been bought, which I checked and paid promptly at the end of the month. But suddenly there were items which I did not order: a brand of cigarettes which I did not smoke, stockings and other small items. When I remonstrated with the merchant, I was told that Leonard had said I had forgotten them from my list. This was worrying. I trusted Leonard implicitly and I knew that he did not smoke. On questioning him, I found that he had a girl-friend who had persuaded him to buy the items. I told him that this time I would pay for his purchases, but he must never do such a thing again. I explained to him that I could not afford to pay for his girl-friend's luxuries. He was quite upset and promised not to do it again. Unfortunately, he soon had a relapse, and I deducted the extras he had bought from his salary. Soon I found towels and other items missing from the flat and felt that there was no way out but to sack him. By this time, Leonard had become a very good cook and he soon found a catering job at a boarding house. His new employers appreciated him but he was unhappy and asked to come back to us, even though he was now earning more than we had paid him. But, reluctantly, I decided to be firm. Nevertheless, Leonard often visited us and we remained good friends.

Before Leonard, I had several helpers but none really suitable, until the arrival of Tamara. She was an attractive black woman, perhaps 28 or 30 years old. She was keen and capable, but there was something odd about her: she was often brought and fetched by someone in a big car – certainly not usual for a South African nanny. We thought she was a real gem – most obliging and always willing to baby-sit. Ilan often said, 'I love Tamara', and we were happy that we had found someone so congenial. Then, Ilan, who was just over three years old at the time, began to scream in his sleep, and it was obvious that he was terrified of something. We did not understand what had happened to him and why he had these nightmares. We could get nothing out of him; so we decided to take him to a child-guidance clinic for help. A charming young therapist by the name of Veronica took him on and started play-therapy with him. It took only two or three sessions for her to discover the cause of his distress. Apparently, Tamara had brought her boyfriend(s) along when she was baby-sitting. She believed in early sex education for

Ilan and woke him and let him watch when she had sex. In the afternoons she would lock him up and hit him. She also taught him to say, 'I love Tamara' and threatened him that if he told anyone what she was doing, he would die. The poor child was terrified. I dismissed her immediately after berating her for what she had done to the child. She did not seem to take it much to heart. After Tamara's departure, my neighbours told me how cruel she had been to Ilan. I wondered why they had not told me this before.

There was another consequence of Tamara's departure. I tried to replace her, but everyone I engaged left screaming a few hours after beginning work. We did not understand why. At last, one of the persons I employed told me that we had black magic in the flat, but refused to tell us where. For many months afterwards I could not get anyone to help me. Then I tried again. I must have wiped off the black-magic sign without knowing it, for the 'spell' was broken. But for Ilan the damage was done and we were most disturbed at what had happened to the boy. The only good thing that came out of poor Ilan's misadventure was friendship with the analyst Veronica, which persists to this very day.

One of the big problems was Ilan's fear of his father. Stephan had no patience with him. He never hit Ilan, but glowered at him, and the look frightened the child. There was always tension between them – a tension that lasted throughout the years. Ilan wanted to learn to play the violin, and Stephan began to teach him. This made me very happy, because I thought the lessons might bring them closer together. We had only returned to South Africa because Stephan was Ilan's father, and now there was this unbearable tension. Stephan would make a fuss of every little girl of our acquaintance, but never bought a present for Ilan or had a kind word for him. The violin lessons were not at all successful. Ilan began to play a little and could produce a reasonable tone quality, except that it was musically completely unconvincing. He never managed successfully to play a single musical phrase. It was quite painful, but although Ilan really hated his lessons, he would not give up. There was a block somewhere and it applied to the only two things Stephan and I had in common: namely music and the Hungarian language. Ilan could not bear to hear Hungarian spoken. Yet he was an extremely good and easy child who was

126

never bored, always busy, and always interested. I could take him to friends and I had no trouble when I spoke French or Hebrew or German, anything as long as it was not Hungarian, which, for him, was like a red rag to a bull. Whenever he heard the language spoken he would throw a tantrum and become quite unbearable. And the same often happened with music: he could not tolerate it.

At school, Ilan was head and shoulders above other pupils, even though he was the youngest in his class. As his relationship with Stephan deteriorated, and the tension increased, I was advised to send him to a boarding school. I met a charming couple who ran such an establishment, King's School, in Nottingham Road, Natal, and I decided to enrol Ilan there. I was very upset at being separated from him once again, but his negative relationship with Stephan left me no choice. We had to pay for Ilan's tuition but we could not afford to pay the full fees. Luckily, these were reduced to accommodate us. Since I missed him as much as I expected to, I visited him often.

Ilan was then not quite seven and I hoped that I had made the right decision in sending him away to school. I still do not know if I did the right thing. Stephan always left all the decisions to me. How often have I since asked myself whether or not I made the right decision? I considered the situation with the greatest care, but realise with hindsight that I could not have radically altered things. All I know is that my decisions were always made for what I thought was best for Ilan.

King's School was set in the middle of spacious grounds and since the intake was not all that large the boys were accorded a great deal of personal attention. Ilan soon jumped another class, which meant he was now two years ahead of his age group. The rapid elevation did not matter that much, for the classes were not separated from each other. Ilan seemed to be happy at the school. But one of his weaknesses was his refusal to participate in the games he thought he might not win. When, on his first Saturday at the school he was invited to play cricket, Ilan told the headmaster that he would not do so. The headmaster replied that if he did not wish to play, he could be a spectator. So he went and watched with the headmaster and soon complained: 'I am not even playing'. The headmaster told him that perhaps next time he would play and so he did. Indeed, he became a most enthusiastic cricketer and turned out to be, according to his next school report, 'a reasonable bat', whatever that meant. Alas, after all these years, understanding or enjoying cricket still eludes me.

Stephan and I were both modest earners, especially by South African standards. But this did not worry us unduly. Throughout my entire life I have never spent quite as much as I had. Even when I was extremely poor, if at all possible I would put a little aside for contingencies. By the middle of 1956, there was some hope that we would soon secure the necessary papers to enable us to move to England, and for this we needed to save. As we had so many friends and kept open house for them, my household expenses soaked up most of our income. Ilan's schooling and the maintenance of the flat were other costly considerations. So I decided that we should give up the flat and move into a modest boarding house. In this way we were able to save up our fares and some money to see us through until we would both be earning again in England.

Stephan had his old Hungarian passport and was able to have it renewed when it expired. However, when I returned my passport for renewal, I was informed that it was not a valid one and should never have been issued to me. Instead of returning my passport, the authorities sent me a letter which stated that I could no longer consider myself a Hungarian citizen. I now had no documents and was definitely stateless, with not even a Nansen passport.[7] When I had gone to Israel, a photograph was stuck on to a piece of paper which served as a document, on which my particulars were typed out and that was the document with which I travelled. While I was in Israel, the new Israeli nationality law had not yet been promulgated, so I could not obtain an Israeli passport and I had returned to South Africa with the same typed document. But this document did not entitle me to go elsewhere (not that I could have afforded to do so). I also had no vote anywhere in the world, although for some years I had been of voting age. It was a most insecure and unpleasant state. By this time (1956) I had my residence and working permits, but I wanted to be a citizen with full political and civil rights. And it was not really South Africa where I wanted to be, but England. At that time, South Africa was still in the Commonwealth, and South African nationality would have entitled us to settle and work in England and eventually to become British nationals.

It might seem callous to use one country to get into another one, but I was in this situation because of my dislike of racial discrimination. I could not make excuses for a country in which racial discrimination existed. And it was quite painful to live in a situation where one could not speak freely. I wanted the required document, and to get it I had to keep silent on what I saw and heard. Most of our friends were politically involved and consequently banned from following their profession, and some had even been jailed as a result of the notorious Treason Trial.[8] Riots in Durban were cunningly manipulated by the government to ensure that the blacks attacked the Indians rather than the whites. In spite of the fact that South Africa had been very good to me, I wanted to get out. If I could not go to Israel where my heart pulled me, then England was my choice. But the papers to emigrate were not forthcoming. On inquiring through influential friends, I learned that the reason for the delay was Stephan's irresponsible driving!

Stephan had a Belgian colleague who was always a great help whenever we were in trouble. But he had one failing – he could not resist an opportunity to make money and when tempted by its lure, friendship went out of the window. He saw the opportunity of making a small profit by 'flogging' the car of a friend and persuaded Stephan to buy it. It was supposed to be a surprise for me, but Stephan could not drive. He had a few driving lessons, but became impatient and, without having passed his test, began driving around in a most irresponsible way. It was terrifying seeing him demonstrate that he could drive without holding the wheel, and he would also perform other daredevil tricks. Once, when I was not at home, he took Ilan in the car and barely managed to stop at the edge of a precipice. It was completely crazy and frightening, but there was no way to stop him. The car possessed him. He finally wrecked it together with another person's vehicle. Luckily, no injuries resulted from this incident, but he now had a police record for driving without a licence, which not only banned him from driving but also prejudiced the granting of our naturalisation.

The usual procedure for becoming naturalised is residence in a country for five years or more. Stephan had been in South Africa since 1947 and I had first gone there in 1948. It was now 1957. We should have received our naturalisation papers long before. Once I had ascertained the reason for the delay, I got some friends to pull strings and we eventually received our papers in July 1957. Now we waited for our South African passports, which took another three weeks. A ship, the *Bloemfontein*, left for England four days later and we were on it.

The last four days were hectic: packing, farewell parties, a farewell concert where Stephan played and farewell ceremonies at my schools. The *Natal Mercury* interviewed us and friends and pupils came with gifts to the ship to bid us farewell. It was very exciting and at the same time rather sad and worrying. Again we were breaking our ties and moving on.

Ilan was extremely upset at leaving South Africa. He had his own friends and was also attached to some of our adult acquaintances, even though he was always something of an outsider. Other children had grandparents, uncles, aunts and cousins. He had none, and he missed that very much. But at least he had friends and now he had to leave them behind. In his short and insecure life this was another upheaval. On the ship he was extremely restless and subjected us to many tantrums. We made friends with a delightful couple, Jack and Stella. Stella was English and Jack South African. Ilan became quite attached to them. It was the beginning of a friendship which has lasted ever since.

On our arrival at Waterloo Station in London, we had, in addition to our trunks, 32 parcels. As we had left in such haste, I had had very little time for packing, and the gifts presented to us added greatly to the luggage. I was never very good at packing and Stephan did not help at all. Friends had rented a room for us in West Hampstead and at Waterloo we stood in a queue waiting for a taxi to take us to our new abode. When a policeman approached us we were apprehensive: having lived in Hungary, France and South Africa, where the police usually were not one's friends, we did not know what would happen. But the policeman said he assumed that we were new immigrants and asked if we knew where we wanted to go. When we told him that we were going to an address in West Hampstead, he suggested that we agree with the taxi-driver on the fare in advance – all the more so, because the distance was more than six miles. In 1957, in London, a driver was permitted to charge anything for a journey in excess of six miles. We were absolutely delighted. We had arrived in a civilised country where even the policemen were decent human beings!

11 • Settling in London

When we arrived in England at the beginning of September, the new school year started. We quickly enrolled Ilan in a school that had been recommended to us and began to look for accommodation in the vicinity.

In West Hampstead we had a pleasant, clean room, sharing the kitchen and bathroom with one other person. We soon began looking for permanent accommodation, not an easy task with the princely sum of £550, our total savings. We had been advised to buy rather than rent. An estate agent who had been recommended to us called to say they might have just the right flat for us. On the following day they showed me a pleasant three-room maisonette about five minutes' walk from Ilan's school. It was on the second floor, with plenty of light, and on a main road, which did not unduly disturb me. I always slept better when there was noise outside and Stephan slept anywhere. I was enchanted. The agent sent me to see the owner of the flat.

Mr F. was very friendly. He had heard that my husband was a musician, and asked if he would make music in the flat. I told him that Stephan was very disciplined and would not practise in the evening after 10 pm, or at times when he might disturb the neighbours. Mr F. told me it would not matter; Stephan could play as much as he liked. Then he wanted to know if we had pets. I said that we had none, but that Ilan had always wanted a cat. He said that he had no objection to pets; little boys should have pets. Of course little boys were themselves noisy animals. I told him that our Ilan was a very quiet boy, but the owner assured me that he would not mind at all if Ilan was noisy.

We also spoke of the fact that I had been in an extermination camp during part of the war and that this would be the first home which we would own. I mentioned that I taught Hebrew. Mr F. was absolutely charming. He said that I would need to have a bridging loan for a brief period, but he would provide that for me and we could have the flat. It cost £3,000, and we paid a deposit of £300. We were told we could move in within two weeks and a date was fixed. At this point, we gave notice to the owners of the room which we occupied. But to our disappointment the maisonette was not ready to move into at the promised time.

Meanwhile, our room had already been let to a new tenant and we had to move. Decent lodgings at a reasonable rent were very scarce. For an entire week we spent every day looking in vain for accommodation. On the morning of the day we had to vacate the room, we found another room, not very far away. But what a come-down! It was a ground-floor room in one of the old houses in West End Lane and was of vast proportions. It must have been the reception room of a well-to-do upper middle-class family, judging from the furniture. There was a table which could be opened to seat 24 people and two glass-fronted bookcases reaching almost to the very high ceiling. One bookcase was white with gold decoration and two larger than life-size human figures on each side. The other case was brown, gilded and with what had once been red plush lining. They were both locked. There was a very large Venetian mirror hanging on the wall which, like everything in the room, was covered with cobwebs and dust, and impossible to reach or clean without a ladder. There was also an assortment of chairs, some very attractive, and in one corner a locked baby grand piano.

For our comfort, there were three bedsteads: one iron, one large heavy Victorian work, brown and carved, and the third painted white and very rickety. For cooking there was a single gas-ring on the floor and a one-bar gas-fire in the fireplace for heating. The gas-fire made hardly any difference to the temperature of this enormous room, except for gobbling up pennies with which we had to feed the meter. The bathroom, on the second floor, was shared by no fewer than 32 people. The filth that had accumulated there was indescribable. The bathroom was a constant source of friction and irritation for its many occupants. It was now the end of October, our first winter after South Africa; it was cold, foggy, damp and extremely unpleasant from the middle of November to the beginning of January, when we were finally able to move. We were utterly miserable during the weeks we waited to occupy our flat.

Finally the day dawned when we were able to move in. The companies to which we had to pay our mortgage payments seemed to change hands quite frequently but it did not really make any difference to us. We were regular payers and had no other business with the companies. It turned out that we were the first to buy a flat in that building. The other flats were let on a lease and the leases were not reaching their end. The owners wanted to sell all the flats and therefore hoped that the present occupants would move out. We were potentially useful to the proprietor – a musician who made a lot of noise, a little boy he hoped would be naughty and noisy, and pets would cause a nuisance to the other occupants. We did not realise that the owners had such expectations of us and we certainly did not live up to our anticipated nuisance value.

As it happened, if we had had the money we would have moved away. The people in the flat below us were jazz musicians. Before we moved in, no-one had occupied our flat for two years. When we arrived we had no money to buy a carpet and walked on the bare boards. Stephan was a heavy man and when he walked every step could be heard below. The musicians resented our being above them and proceeded to make our lives impossible. Every movement in our flat provoked knocking on the ceiling of their flat. When Ilan came home they would waylay him and threaten and frighten him. When I complained to the National Society for the Prevention of Cruelty to Children, the jazz musicians retaliated by playing music loudly and banging on the drums until 1 or 2 am. It was unbearable and we had no peace.

One night, when it really became too much and we were quite desperate, we called the police. It was 1.30 in the morning and they were playing their jazz pieces at full volume. A policeman came and agreed that it was an impossible situation. He said he would like to help us. When he asked how many of the people living in the flats complained, we told him that we were the only ones affected by the loud music. The flat below that of the jazz musicians had been empty for a long time and sound did not carry sideways. Hence, we were the only ones affected by the noise. The policeman explained that we had little chance of redress because, according to the law, three tenants had to complain for a complaint to be valid. Nevertheless, he promised to see what he could do. He would speak to the tenants below and get back to us. When the police constable returned he told us that he had informed the people below that legal steps might be taken against them. The threat was sufficient and for a time we had peace.

Many years later there was a rent racket scandal in London: the Rachman affair. The 'slum landlord' Rachman was notorious for exploiting tenants and driving them out by devious means in order to sell his properties at inflated prices. When the list of the mortgage companies was made known we found that Rachman controlled all the companies to which we had been paying our mortgage.

We had come to England with several contacts through whom Stephan could resume work. However, he seemed to ruin almost every meeting with these people. Whether he did so on purpose, or invariably behaved awkwardly to disguise some shyness or embarrassment, I never knew. Every time we met people who wanted to help him, but who asked for details of his background and professionalism, Stephan somehow managed to irritate them, and again I was at the end of my tether.

We also made contact with some old friends from Hungary. During 1940 or 1941 in Szombathely we were preparing a performance of Handel's oratorio, 'Judas Maccabaeus'. As I was a member of the choir and of the orchestra it was decided that for half the performance I should play cello in the orchestra and for the other half sing in the choir. We waited for the conductor and soloists to arrive. The conductor was László Weiner, a native of Szombathely then living in Budapest. He was a gifted musician and the favourite pupil of the Hungarian composer, Zoltán Kodály. I had known him and his family since childhood. When home on holiday, he often paid a visit to my father, with whom he became very friendly. On that occasion he brought with him his fiancée, Vera Rózsa, a gifted and beautiful young singer. Vera had the most exquisite mezzo-soprano voice and I became her devotee from the moment I first heard her perform. From then on, she often came to town for *Lieder* recitals. They were a great pleasure. Vera's voice, musicality and charm were irresistible. My knowledge was

135

considerably enhanced as a result of Vera's extensive repertory of folksongs from many countries.

During the war Vera was in hiding. Laci Weiner had been taken into a Hungarian labour camp with other Jewish men of military age and although Kodály tried all he could to get him released, by the time he had succeeded, Laci was dead in the Ukraine where Jews were used as guinea-pigs on minefields or died of cold and starvation. While I lived in Budapest between 1942 and 1944, I never missed a concert where Vera sang and she was always a delightful friend. She certainly was the darling of the entire Jewish musical world in Hungary and was praised by Gentile Hungarians even when she was not permitted to perform in non-Jewish circles during these war years.

After the war Vera married Ralph Nordell, an Englishman who was in Hungary with the British Army. For a while she performed at the Budapest and Vienna opera houses with such great conductors as Otto Klemperer and Josef Krips. She and her husband then moved to Italy and from there to London. When we settled in London, Vera and Ralph were my main support. At the time she was slowly winning acclaim in England, and she went on to become an internationally recognised singing-teacher, honoured everywhere. She conducts master-classes throughout the world and is today in great demand as a judge at international competitions.

To return to my endeavours to get Stephan settled in England, we finally had a stroke of luck. Once again, our good friend, the Hungarian cellist, János Starker, came to our aid. He was in London to perform at a concert and to record with the Philharmonia. I went to a Haydn cello concerto recording which he was making with the conductor, Giulini. What a joy it was to hear him again! It was extremely difficult to get an audition with the Philharmonia, which by then had become one of the world's great orchestras, but Janos arranged an audition for Stephan. As a result he was offered a place by Walter Legge as a viola player and remained with the orchestra for 27 years.

I was also attempting to secure employment as a Hebrew teacher. I had excellent recommendations from my former headmaster in South Africa, Mr Ernst, and from the Jewish education inspector there, Mr Goss, who commended my work at the Durban Jewish schools. Mr Ernst knew that although I was not religious, I respected other people's sincere beliefs and would never attempt to undermine those who held strong conviction. I always felt that he was pleased with my work and there was mutual respect between us.

In London, the United Synagogue educational authorities, to which I made an approach, questioned me about my private life. They asked whether I travelled on the Sabbath and whether they could inspect my kitchen for *kashrut*.[9] I refused to accept such an invasion of my privacy and turned to the Zionist education board, but they would only employ Israelis. I was, however, offered work at the Reform Synagogue, but only on Sundays, which was insufficient to provide me with an adequate income. But after due consideration, I accepted employment with the Reform Synagogue and enjoyed working there. Later, I was able to teach at a Hebrew class in the late afternoon during the week.

But I still needed to earn money for our sustenance and I was willing to accept anything – not for the first time. The first job I obtained was as a ledger clerk at a roof manufacturing firm. I had never seen a ledger before, but it did not take me long to get the hang of it. The books were three months behind and it took me two weeks to update them. I worked four hours a day, but travelling to and from the company often took two hours. For my labour (in January 1958), I was paid the princely sum of three shillings and sixpence an hour (18p in present-day money).

After the first two weeks, I hardly had any work. I sat in a room where the accounts and salaries were dealt with. There must have been overmanning, for the four people who were in the room worked only when the door opened and someone came in from another office. I would complete the work as soon as I got it and I then sat and twiddled my thumbs. My office colleagues tried to persuade me to go slow, so that it would seem as if there was plenty to do. The tea-kettle was kept busy throughout the day and the conversation was quite unbearable. Perhaps I was a snob, but the incessant use of four-letter words jarred painfully on my ears. Indeed, some 50 per cent of the office chatter consisted of four-letter profanities. One of the employees was a self-styled expert on murder and read only newspapers which printed all the gory details. He would then analyse them and compare them with other murders committed over the past 60 years. I really found the environment difficult to bear and decided I could not spend much more time in it.

I met someone from the BBC who was interested in my knowledge of languages and invited me to work for her. But the job description required a knowledge of shorthand and I had none. She attempted to persuade her superiors that shorthand was really not needed for the position, but to no avail; rules were rules.

Nevertheless, this setback inspired me to learn shorthand. Meanwhile, I had moved up from ledger clerk to writing addresses at a new post with the Advance Laundry. The work was no better than my previous job but at least it was closer to home and I spent less time travelling.

First I began to learn Speedwriting and became reasonably proficient at typing. But I was unable to achieve any great speed, and so I could not obtain a certificate of proficiency. Consequently no employment agency would take me on. I spent some three months trying to improve my Speedwriting, but at every test I collapsed in tears and nervousness. Finally, I was asked to leave the class, since I was apparently demoralising the others. So I sadly gave up trying to become a first-class speedwriter.

Someone suggested that as I could now at least type, another method of transcription might suit me better. It was called Palantype, a form of shorthand by machine, taught at another business school. Again I was quick to learn the technique but unable to pass a reasonable speed test. I got friendly with the instructors, one of whom offered me the opportunity to train as a teacher. But they could only promise me evening class work in the event of my training being satisfactory.

As I wanted to be at home with Ilan in the evening, there was no point in contemplating evening work. I had spent quite a lot of money on business school education seemingly with little result. Just before I left the Palantype school, one of the older pupils (now living in Israel) came to visit. She asked whether the same method might be applied for Hebrew instruction in Israel. There were already German and French methods and my teachers thought this

138

an interesting suggestion. Since they knew that I spoke Hebrew and was fully conversant with the method, they offered to return my tuition fee if I would edit the Hebrew method for them. This I did to my great satisfaction.

At the same time I utilised one of my old skills: singing. I had an audition with a synagogue and was accepted as usual for the choir. I was not religious and would not have attended synagogue had I not been paid to do so as a member of the choir. This particular Orthodox synagogue was not supposed to have a mixed choir and whenever the Chief Rabbi came on a visit, the female members were paid not to come.

In the Advance Laundry, also writing addresses, there was a Czech Jewish refugee who had also been in an extermination camp. We became quite friendly. One day, as we left together and queued for the bus, in front of us stood a black woman. When it came to our turn to board the bus, my Czech colleague pushed past her, telling her that, as she was coloured she should let others in the queue go in front of her! I was horrified and told her so. I never spoke to her again. That a Jewess who had suffered because of racial discrimination could behave like that was for me quite unbearable and repugnant.

Meanwhile, someone suggested that I might like to work in a library. I was thrilled at the idea. I was sent to the Wiener Library (the London research library specialising in the Holocaust), but unfortunately there was no position available. During the interview I was offered a small sum to write an eyewitness report on my deportation from Hungary. I was given a report to read as an example of what was required. The report was by a cellist from Germany who had been in the Auschwitz extermination camp orchestra. She was now married to the fine pianist, Peter Wallfisch, and, as it happened, we had visited them only a few days earlier. I always had a good memory for faces and when we visited the Wallfisches, I seemed to remember Anita's face. But there seemed no way we could have met, or so I thought. Now, from her eyewitness report, I realised that she was the cellist I had spoken to the day before we were taken away from Auschwitz.

I was still trying to obtain a full-time teaching position, but the nearest I got was a job as school secretary at the Hasmonean

Grammar School for Girls. I found the headmistress, Mrs Phyllis Dimson, a most delightful person, and we got on well together. When I assumed my duties, the office was in a complete mess. I soon reorganised it and then even had time to help some of the girls with their French or German studies and their personal problems. I soon knew every child by name and they came to me with their little stories. I also rendered first aid. I enjoyed my work, even though the pay was poor and the job entitled me to only two weeks' holiday a year. I felt I was being exploited. Then, when the director of the school was offered the services of the daughter of a friend, a young girl who had just completed her typing course and was willing to take the job at one pound less than I earned (seven pounds a week!), I was sacked one Monday morning and told to leave by the end of the week. The new 'secretary' lasted only three weeks and, I heard, was absolutely incapable of fulfilling her duties. Mrs Dimson fought for me, but to no avail; I left feeling very cross and upset. For many years afterwards I would come across old school girls and we enjoyed our friendly chat. An amusing example of my high reputation with the girls was when one eleven-year-old believed that I could help cure her chilblains where her doctor could not. I had to disappoint her.

Not long after losing my job at the school, I had a call from the Wiener Library to say that they had a position for me as an assistant to the librarian. She told me that she was considering working only part-time and she would train me to take over when she was not available. I enrolled for evening classes in librarianship at the North Western Polytechnic and completed a year's introductory course. As far as I know, my teacher thought highly of me but, as usual, when it came to examinations I just managed to scrape through. I very much enjoyed the course. I also quite enjoyed the work at the library and found it extremely interesting, though somewhat harrowing. Its emphasis was on the history of Nazism and the Holocaust and, as the only person on the library staff who had survived the concentration camps, I felt I was being used as a guinea-pig supplying information to journalists.

By this time my personal life had again become quite complicated. Ilan was very unhappy at his new school. He had been put back into his own age-group and was bored. Until then he had always been in small classes of twelve pupils at most. Suddenly he was in a class of 45 children with a teacher who had neither the time nor the imagination to deal with a bright child.

In South Africa Ilan had been an avid reader and used often to go to the public library. Poetry books were his special delight. If he liked a poem he would memorise it and do all kinds of illustrations for it. While reciting poems, he would draw or paint or mould plasticine or dough or make shapes from sand or even from cardboard, or wood to illustrate them. In Durban, he had a large table in his room which he painted to give the impression of fields, forests and gardens. These he populated with animals and country-folk, together with farm implements and farm houses cut out of paper. He began this novel enterprise from the age of four and went on with it until he was just over eight when we left Durban. During the holidays he attended art classes and his work was considered so exceptional that just before we left South Africa, an entire room at an exhibition was devoted to his creations.

He was such a cheerful little fellow, but now, in his new school, things began to change for him. When his teacher asked him to recite a poem, he did so gladly. When he had finished, she told him it was not a suitable poem for a little boy. After this experience he never read another poem until he was a university student. The same thing occurred when he was asked to draw a tree; the teacher did not like it, and he never drew another line. He was utterly miserable and became irritable and cross and got involved in fights with the other children. He was terribly lonely, for although he made friends, at weekends his friends were with their relatives and he had none. He began bed-wetting and having nightmares.

Once again I called on our friend Veronica, who now lived in London and studied with Anna Freud. She arranged for Ilan to be seen at the Anna Freud clinic where, following some tests, he was found to have an IQ of 167. It was quite obvious that his major problem at school was sheer boredom, though there was also the old problem of his unhappy relationship with Stephan.

Two years passed and Ilan got increasingly worse. He bitterly disliked school and, at the Freud clinic, we were advised to put him into a school where he would be permitted to work and advance at his own pace. Dartington Hall was mentioned. By this time, he had secured a place at the Haberdashers' School, but we were advised against enrolling him there. The clinic thought that, as he was so very bright, too much pressure might be put on him for scholastic achievement. They suggested that it would be best for Ilan to attend a school which offered a greater variety of courses and activities and where classes were smaller.

And so I went with him to the Dartington Hall School, in South Devon, and we were delighted with what we found there. Ilan was thrilled, for he had the possibility of spending some time on the farm attached to the school. He had always enjoyed being on farms and in South Africa would help collect eggs, feed the animals, clean the pens and do anything and everything.

Dartington seemed to me to be a children's paradise. There were laboratories, a library, an art-studio and a theatre where the children could use all the equipment and give free range to their imaginations. They were also allowed to keep pets. There were facilities for most sports. The idea was that if you put an intelligent child into such an environment, he or she would choose and find the right place in society. Unfortunately, this notion did not quite work at the time Ilan was at the school. Children do need some framework of discipline; very few can maintain their own routine and not 'go overboard' as Ilan did.

At the lower level at Dartington there were some compulsory subjects, but later the choice of all subjects was made entirely free. Examinations were frowned upon. The rooms were pleasant and the entire school was situated in the most salubrious surroundings. But it was an expensive school and, since we were still struggling with our mortgage payments (we also had a second mortgage), we could afford very little else. Although delighted with the school, I pointed out that it was beyond our means. Consequently, we were elated when, within a few days of our visit to Dartington, we had a letter informing us that Ilan had been awarded a scholarship and a grant and had received a completely free place from the Elms' Trust. Ilan was also delighted and very keen to become a boarder at Dartington.

Since our settling in London, Ilan had often been ill. He had had a ruptured spleen which fortunately surgery had taken care of, and he had had his tonsils removed. The Ear Nose and Throat Hospital, where the latter operation was performed, rather puzzled me. As usual, the day before the operation Ilan was not supposed to eat anything, but the operation was delayed some 24 hours and again he had nothing at all to eat. By the time he was operated on and brought some food, 48 hours had elapsed. What did a specialist hospital serve to a child with a very empty stomach after a tonsillectomy? Baked beans on toast! The poor boy had such cramps that he hardly felt the pain in his throat. Was that the reason for such treatment? I felt terribly sorry for him. Afterwards he was allowed the customary ice-cream, but by then the damage was done. He also had various other ailments and was constantly in and out of hospital. It was indeed time for him to go to the country for healthier surroundings.

At Dartington he was in the junior school at first – he was not yet eleven at the time – and he was very happy. All the children were required to do some work on the estate and Ilan spent at least an hour a day helping out on his beloved farm. He also began woodwork and built a hutch for two rabbits. I had a letter from the school asking if he could have the rabbits as pets. I readily agreed until the housemother warned me that he would have to bring the rabbits home during his school holidays. Since we did not think it a good idea to keep rabbits in a second-floor flat, I bargained with Ilan.

He already had a tabby cat, whose name in full was Timothy Maccabee Deak, shortened to Timmy. We had given it to Ilan for the first Chanukkah festival we spent in the flat and all of us got great pleasure out of this beautiful, affectionate little creature who was terrified to venture out. Of course, the cat remained at home when Ilan went off to Dartington. We had also had the company of a golden hamster which Veronica had presented to Ilan for his birthday. It was a sweet little animal and Veronica maintained that there was no need to keep it in a cage. She had kept the animal in her wardrobe for a few days before presenting it to Ilan, and assured us that the hamster was a tame friendly creature. I did not quite believe her and confined the animal to a cage. When Veronica next wanted to put on her expensive and beautiful woollen dress she realised why the hamster had been so docile; it had been extremely busy gnawing holes in her best frock!

Now in place of rabbits Ilan accepted goldfish, terrapins, a budgerigar and two mice. Decidedly, it was a compromise. When we went to the railway station to see him off after the holidays, some of the children had parrots and one of them even had a monkey. What a sight Ilan was at the station! On his backpack was a wooden box containing the mice. On his arm were jars containing the terrapins and the goldfish. In front, suspended from his neck, hung the birdcage. Later a fishing rod was added for he became keen on trout fishing. When all these animals came home there was always much interest from Timmy, the cat, and we had to watch him very carefully. The important thing was that it made Ilan happy.

I could visit Ilan only once a term. The train journey to Dartington, the overnight stay and taking him out to meals added up to a considerable expense. Such a weekend would cost as much as £25, a princely sum at the time, since my weekly salary at the Wiener Library was a mere £9. Most of the other parents, who were obviously well-to-do, came in Rolls Royces and Bentleys or expensive sports cars. Ilan began to feel this disparity between his family and his classmates' parents very intensely and it soon became a problem. He started to spend his savings, though the school did not allow pupils to have more than a certain amount of pocket money (which, naturally, Ilan received from us). It was obvious that this rule was not adhered to by the other parents. But equally disturbing was the fact that Ilan began to tell lies. He was developing in a way that made me unhappy. It was apparent that he found it difficult, being a scholarship boy amidst all this affluence. Yet he advanced in his studies at such a rate that he was moved up twice, jumping classes.

Ilan's classmates were now much older than he and not so keen on getting on with their studies. Ilan was extremely ambitious, to the point where he had to be first in everything. He excluded himself completely from extra-curricular activities – art, drama, music – to concentrate solely on study. His teachers gave him no encouragement. Many years later, I heard from Ian, one of his classmates, that he had also been subjected to anti-Semitism. (Ian became his best friend when they met up after they both left Dartington.) Ilan stopped working on the farm; he had mainly looked after pigs, cleaning out the sties and feeding the animals before his breakfast. The smell of his endeavours lingered on his person and no-one wanted to sit next to him. Nevertheless, he left Dartington, hardly 17 years old, with eight O-levels, four A-levels and two Scholarship-levels, and all at top grade. But he had not made one friend, and had ignored all the extra-curricular activities on offer. Still, we felt fortunate, since so many of his generation had become involved in drugs, stolen cars and indulged in other dangerous exploits. Many of Ilan's classmates had to go on at the age of 19 to an adult education college to study for exams because of their failure to do anything constructive during their last years at Dartington. It was sad that such a marvellous concept as Dartington exemplified lacked the fulfilment. Although Ilan's last years at the school were not very happy, he did not want to leave. When he did, he was in a hurry to go on to university.

12 • *Looking for love*

I was now working five days a week at the Wiener Library, and on Sunday mornings and one late afternoon I taught at my local Reform Synagogue. I had left the synagogue choir as soon as I had a job I felt would be permanent. Once a week I went to Library School at the North Western Polytechnic. One evening a week I went to sing in the Philharmonia Choir, a great honour for me since by repute it was the best choir in England and, indeed, one of the best in the world. It was formed under the auspices of the Philharmonia Orchestra, which was managed by Walter Legge, who brought to London the most prestigious conductors and soloists. The choir practised under the baton of Wilhelm Pitz, who was the choir-master for the Bayreuth Festival, and he flew over from Germany once a week for rehearsals.

When I auditioned for the choir, I was very nervous. It was the first time I had had to audition with songs and not just scales and arpeggios. Pitz was not interested in whether I could read music, still less sight-read. Perhaps, as most singers in the choir were professional or at least semi-professional, he assumed that I could read music. I sang songs by Schubert which I knew reasonably well, but as I had never had a singing lesson in my life my performance was obviously amateurish. Pitz's only objection to my *Lieder* was my choice: they were all for the male voice. They included Schubert's 'Wegweiser', 'Ihr Bild' and 'Irrlicht'. I had chosen them because I found them easier to sing as they were slow in tempo. But they did reflect the range of my voice which was of fair compass, and I was delighted to be accepted.

We sang Verdi's 'Requiem' with Giulini and performed it at the 1960 Edinburgh Festival. It was a great joy to sing with Giulini; he was always so polite and charming and friendly. This could not be said of Sir Thomas Beecham with whom we had presented

Handel's 'Messiah' at the Lucerne Festival the previous year. He was most uncivil, apparently because he had a grudge against Walter Legge and seemed determined to ruin the performance. He had already spoiled the dress-rehearsal, which was public and which was offered as a reward to all the good people who had hosted members of the choir for four nights. We found Beecham's attitude mean-minded.

The choir also recorded Beethoven's Ninth (Choral) Symphony with Otto Klemperer. It was exciting to work with him; he hardly moved his hands. Klemperer was far from attractive to behold but had once been handsome: he had suffered a stroke and had roughed up his appearance by stepping out of an aeroplane before the steps were properly in position. Yet he had such charisma that he was able to elicit anything he wanted both from the choir and the orchestra. I was sometimes moved to tears by the beauty and serenity he managed to generate. The choir also performed Beethoven's Ninth with Hindemith, who was a far better composer than conductor but a real gentleman. Under Wolfgang Sawallisch's sympathetic baton we performed Borodin's 'Polovtsian Dances' in Russian, after being coached by a Russian journalist. Another real gentleman was William Walton, with whom we performed and recorded his 'Belshazzar's Feast'. The choir also presented Beethoven's 'Missa Solemnis' and Brahms's 'Ein deutsches Requiem', both conducted by Klemperer. It was indeed invigorating to take part in such performances.

I knew several professional choristers who were unable to get any work and was concerned that we amateurs might deprive them of their livelihood. However, as Stephan was working with the Philharmonia, I felt I could say nothing. Later, we were required to attend two or even three rehearsals a week, and so singing with the choir became too much for me. I left the Philharmonia with some regrets but it was necessary to work out my priorities. Meanwhile, I had acquired several private pupils whom I taught in the evenings, on Saturdays and even on Sundays. At the Sunday school I achieved good results, but it involved twelve hours a week preparing for the two-and-a-half-hour classes. At the same time I began a relationship which was to last for the next eight years.

My marriage now consisted solely of managing and maintaining

Stephan's household. We were becoming ever more estranged. I did try to make the best of our marriage, but felt increasingly unhappy. I could easily have had some attachment, but most of the men I met were married and I was determined never again to get involved with anyone in that position. The last thing I desired was to ruin someone else's married life.

At the Wiener Library I met Dr Franta Hajek, who came originally from Czechoslovakia. He was 22 years older than I and seemed to be a confirmed bachelor. His marriage, which lasted only for a year, had been contracted in the hope that his girl-friend, a German refugee in Czechoslovakia, would be saved from the Nazis if she was Czech and not a German national. But when Czechoslovakia was occupied by the Germans, it was of no avail; she managed to escape to France and he to Italy. The separation terminated their relationship and she eventually married another man. Hajek was a wonderful person but not without his peculiarities. He told me that at his wedding he had played cards the entire night and had then met his wife for breakfast at a coffee-house. He never permitted her to cook because he was a gourmet and did not believe that a mere woman could cook a decent meal. He always ate in first-class restaurants in Prague where the chefs and waiters knew and spoiled him. Although by profession a lawyer, Hajek spent most of his time reading, and associated with writers, journalists and actors. He possessed a phenomenal memory and most of his writer friends would ask him to read their manuscripts for errors. These tasks he gladly accepted as a labour of love.

Following his escape to Italy, he was interned in a camp. Concentration camps in that country were not run by Nazi sadists and he was not treated too badly. He quickly learned to speak faultless Italian without any accent. After the liberation, he was with the Allied armies in Italy and made many friends. In the post-war years he was appointed Cultural Attaché at the Czechoslovak Embassy in Rome, a post which he greatly enjoyed because it again brought him in contact with artists, writers and journalists. Then he was recalled to Prague, but was warned by friends not to return. He did not heed the warnings and on his arrival in the Czech capital, was dismissed from his position and deprived of all of his property, having been denounced by the Communist authorities as a bourgeois cosmopolitan. They sent him to work as a labourer. He managed to escape to Italy, but without a work-permit had a very difficult time.

Hajek had a brother, Ferry, who had come to England before the war. He had taken advantage of a British government scheme whereby any refugee who could establish an industry in a depressed area, and thus provide work for the unemployed, was entitled to assistance. Ferry, who knew much about the manufacture of clothing, established an outstandingly successful children's clothing factory in Maryport, Cumberland, where he employed some 460 people. He soon became quite wealthy and helped his brother Franta in Italy as much as he could. But, after a few years, when it became clear to Franta that there was no future for him in Italy, he emigrated to England. He found employment partly in his brother's office and partly at the Wiener Library. He did not enjoy working for his brother but in the Wiener Library he was very much in his element. He read widely and memorised what he read – and so was able to answer any enquiry very quickly. Many editors of journals, after a conversation with Hajek, invited him to write articles on his observations or do book-reviews. But in spite of his immense knowledge and command of several languages, no-one could get anything from him that could be published. I never understood his reluctance to put pen to paper.

Franta lived in a small room where his landlady made breakfast for him and attended to all his household needs. He refused to go to any shop except for books or drinks. He was a small, rather rotund man with very short legs who, although he would never admit it, suffered an inferiority complex being of diminutive stature. Any man he met who was two inches taller than himself Franta considered handsome and admirable. He was extremely fond of food and drink, especially Italian food and wine. Having travelled in Europe extensively before the war, he remembered the best places to eat in, the specialities of the house, and, last but not least, every painting or sculpture in any museum, gallery or public place. Italy, of course, he knew remarkably well. He managed admission to places not open to the public, especially if there was something worth seeing there. He knew how to make the best of life, and yet he was a lonely and not really a happy man. As he became older he regretted that he had not married when young and that he had no children, because he adored them and often had a charming relationship with them when they were still small. When they became older, they resented being treated by him as if too young to know their own minds. Ilan was very fond of Franta when he was small.

Italy was Franta's great love, and he would return to the country whenever he could. He was in constant correspondence with many authors and well-known people in public life, and through him I met a number of interesting people. Franta had a ready wit and a sparkling repartee. Even today, when poor Franta has been long dead, my present husband Franz and I remember him constantly and often quote his wry, inconsequential observations.

Franta and I became very fond of each other. When I first met him he drank heavily. Indeed, on the first evening we spent together he bought six bottles of Yugoslav slivovitz and during the following six evenings we drank a bottle each night. I did my fair share of the drinking as I could also hold my liquor pretty well. But usually I never drank more than one small glass. This time I kept up with Franta. He was impressed and that had been my aim. After the sixth bottle, I told him that now that I had shown him I could drink as well as he, and it was no big deal, he must cut down his intake drastically or else I would stop seeing him. After that he did stop drinking heavily. Whenever there was a free long weekend, we travelled to Holland or Belgium or Paris.

I learned much from Franta. I was still shy, especially with men, but Franta gave me confidence in myself and made a woman of me with his attentions and devotion. We spent our time together in restaurants or at theatres, concerts, and films, and I was very spoiled. Stephan knew about and accepted the relationship.

However, after several years I found our situation unsatisfactory. Except when we were travelling, which was always sheer joy and highly interesting, the relationship began to pall. Although Franta talked about marriage, he was not cut out for such a relationship. He absolutely refused any of the responsibilities linked with running a home. We could not go to his place and we usually met at a friend's flat when that person was out. It was not a satisfactory situation and, as time passed, I felt that what I really wanted was a settled home life. I was, in the meantime, maintaining a home for Stephan and cooking his meals, even though I hardly ever ate at home. But coffee-houses and restaurants began to pall on me, especially since I enjoy entertaining friends at home, and with Franta that was impossible. Then, too, I tired of his treating me as a piece of property. When he introduced me to his friends, it was only as 'Trude, my girlfriend', without mentioning my surname. This offended me and I told him so, but he seemed not to understand when I said that I had a name and expected to be introduced by it.

I became depressed. At the Wiener Library there was a curious atmosphere; the staff were marvellous in personal relationships. Birthdays were celebrated and when someone fell ill, all were sympathetic and helpful. Yet workwise they seemed to spy on each other and there was a good deal of jealousy among the personnel. As time went on, I found the atmosphere unpleasant and felt that I had to get away from the library. I still enjoyed my work and found it interesting, but with the Eichmann trial, my 'guinea-pig' status became too much for me. I was still paid poorly, earning only £9 a week, though now it was already 1964.

I had some hope of again being employed by the Reform Synagogue as a nursery school teacher. Nothing came of it, but I was offered a position in the library of the Overseas Development Institute, and I left the Wiener Library at Christmas 1964 for my new job. Work at the ODI was pleasant and interesting. I was thrilled to learn about developing countries instead of concentration camps and persecution of the Jews. This was dealing with the future and hope, instead of the morbid past.

In 1967 I took a big decision. I decided that it was my last chance to end my marriage. Stephan seemed to be coping better and I left him alone more and more. Ilan was now no longer a child; having finished at Dartington, he had decided to spend the next three years at home working for his first academic degree at London University. For Oxford or Cambridge he would have had to wait another year; he was only 17 when he was accepted at King's College, London, to read biology. I now spent much time with him, but I felt that he did not really need me except as a friend.

151

Ilan had begun calling himself Alan and decided to change his surname when he came of age. He intended to change it to Davidson. This was quite amusing. His name was Deak, a good Hungarian name, which his grandfather had taken. Many Jews in Hungary, to escape discrimination, had opted for Hungarian names. His grandfather's former name was Davidovits, which meant exactly that: the son of David, hence Davidson. Ilan resented being Jewish and for a long time refused to go out with any Jewish girl. He had developed a strong complex about his Jewishness, which I found sad. I had always accepted my Jewishness (even though I was not observant) and would not have changed or denied it (except when it had really been dangerous in Egypt, in March 1948, without a passport). I believe it was our past that frightened Ilan, but I was unable to have an unemotional conversation with him about his Jewishness. Yet in the end he married a Jewish girl, Isabelle. But at the time he disliked his Hungarian surname and wanted to be like most of his colleagues: English. Later, he realised that it was quite intriguing to have an interesting, uncommon name and, as he was very much an individualist, he abandoned his original name-change.

Ilan was very handsome and, although he should have been successful with girls of his own age, seemed to have no difficulties with older women. The major reason was probably that he was much less developed emotionally than intellectually. He was very clever but did not show it. Yet he could be intolerant and highly critical. He got on extremely well with Dr Emily Jean Hanson, his professor at King's College, who took him to conferences, even in his first year. At such meetings Ilan's searching questions attracted the attention of leading biologists and he had invitations that were usually extended only to doctoral students. More than once he found it difficult to convince academics that he was only a first-year undergraduate.

When Ilan completed his bachelor's degree, he knew exactly where and with whom he would like to undertake his doctoral studies. He always knew what he wanted and always succeeded in getting it. He went to Oxford to see Professor Henry Harris, the professor he wanted to work with, and when he got the place, he asked for it to be held for him for a year. He wanted to take a year off

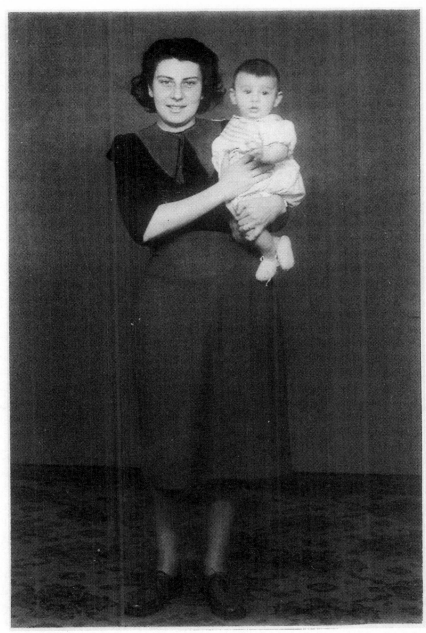

8   Durban, August 1949: With her son Ilan before leaving for Israel

9   London, 1961–64: Working at the Wiener Library

10   With second husband Franz Levi

11   Oxford, 1973: With Ilan at his DPhil degree ceremony

12   London, 1991: With her grandchildren, Jonathan and Marina

from formal studies to travel and study foreign languages. He was still only 20 years old.

With his backpack, Ilan went off on his travels. First I managed to arrange a job for him in Italy, where he worked for Volkswagen in Verona, mainly sweeping the floor of the store where the spare parts were kept. He was there for three months and learned to speak fluent Italian. He had had a similar few weeks with Volkswagen in Wolfsburg in Germany. He already spoke excellent French, quite a bit of Russian (which he had studied), and German. He had tried to learn Hungarian, but was still unable to cope with the language for which he had a psychological block. Mastering Magyar was not to be his forte.

When Ilan was eleven he had wanted to go to France during the holidays to learn French. He had had a few lessons but really knew very little. The day before he left I bought him a small dictionary at Woolworths. Two days later we had the first letter from him, entirely in French. He had translated every word literally with his dictionary! The letter ended 'Amour, Ilan'. The French family with whom he stayed spoke some English, but Ilan absolutely refused to speak anything but French. Seven weeks later he returned home speaking fluent French with an excellent accent.

After Italy, Ilan spent a couple of months in Spain picking fruit and learning Spanish. From Spain he went to Greece to pick grapes and again to learn the language.

By this time I decided to give myself another chance: my priority was now to find another partner for the remainder of my life. I was willing to give up two years in search of a husband. If I did not succeed, I would begin studying for an academic degree to give myself a different aim in life. (I always enjoyed studying, but my behaviour at examinations and the low results I invariably achieved made me reluctant to pursue formal studies.) But life was getting me down. Once I had made this decision, I went for it with all the determination I could muster. Franta was extremely upset, but as I saw that our relationship had become completely unsatisfactory, and was without future, I explained to him that I intended to take my life into my own hands.

I began going to any 'unattached' club advertised in the *New*

Statesman, thinking that I had a better opportunity of meeting someone of my own views and ideas if the person read that particular journal. Every night I went to one of the clubs in search of a new partner.

The first club I attended was organised by a hypnotherapist and we met in the hall of a West End hotel. We were sitting in a circle and a hat was passed round from which each took a piece of paper. On the note was written a word on which each of us was asked to speak for a minute. I was near the end of the circle and could hardly hear what the others were saying for I was so nervous at having to speak in front of some 150 persons. When my turn came I got up, stuttered, and burst into tears. I was quite unable to speak and had to sit down in shame, having failed to make my contribution. I returned to the club almost a year later, before my membership expired. By that time my shyness was gone and I did not hesitate to speak about anything.

The next club I went to was run by a group called Neurotics Anonymous. I thought it was a curious name and somehow did not realise it meant what it purported to be. I certainly did not consider myself neurotic. NA was run by a man called Jack who was blind. We met above a pub and we gave only our forenames. We could give any name we liked as long as we answered to it when asked to speak or answer a question. At the beginning of the evening, four topics were suggested for discussion. Then a vote was taken and one of the four subjects was discussed during the ensuing hour. Anybody could take part in the discussion and if you did not speak, Jack would attempt to draw you into the discussion. With me, however, he had tried for some months, but I rarely came out with more than a 'yes' or a 'no'. After drinks during the interval, Jack would ask if anyone wanted to discuss a personal problem. Mostly the same people spoke; sometimes a person who had never spoken before would suddenly burst out with a problem and all would discuss it. Again I remained silent. During the break or after the meetings I would quite freely discuss all that I had heard with one or at the most two people, but I could not get myself to speak to the entire group. I made quite a few friends at NA and yet I sometimes wondered what I was doing there. There were several seriously disturbed people among the company and I did not feel I had serious emotional problems. Nevertheless, I persevered and returned regularly to the weekly sessions.

One day someone said something that struck a chord in me and suddenly I jumped up and asked to be heard about my personal problems – the remark related to shyness and the feeling that as a child I was always being treated as if I had no brains. I heard myself speaking and speaking and answering questions, delving into my past and present life and discussing my problem. I could hardly believe that it was I talking to all these strangers. I now found that the others listened to what I had to say and discussed it and did not think that what I said was stupid. It was a strange, wonderful sensation. After this experience, I had no difficulty in speaking to a group and henceforth I always actively participated in the discussions. And I could now participate in all that took place in the other clubs. So I returned to the first club, pulled out my word from the hat and spoke for the required minute.

In all of these clubs – except at Neurotics Anonymous, where I came quite by accident – the ratio of women to men was about ten to one. Thus men had the greater choice of women in the groups. Those men who were at all interesting came only once or twice and would then disappear with one of the women. The men who came often had great difficulty entering into, and, even more, maintaining, any kind of relationship. After clubbing practically every night of the week, I noticed that women who ran the clubs had greater opportunities to meet interesting men.

In the spring of 1969 two women advertised in the *New Statesman* stating that they wished to form a new club for unattached Jewish people and invited interested persons to join. I answered the advertisement and was invited to the preliminary meeting of the group. Although there were 48 replies, only twelve were invited to attend the first meeting which was held in a private home. We discussed what sort of a club this would be and we decided to write to all those who had responded to the advertisement to attend the next meeting. I volunteered to serve as secretary and to send out the invitations, and another person offered her home for the next meeting. Since again there were many more women than men, I wrote a note on every woman's invitation asking her to bring an unattached male friend in whom she was not personally interested.

The club met on 14 July 1969 (Bastille Day). When I entered the room there were already quite a number of people present. One of the men came up to me and we had a delightful conversation. Then he moved on to someone else. As the evening progressed, we asked for ideas on how the club might function and the man to whom I had spoken offered so many good ideas that he was asked to serve as president. He accepted the position.

As president and secretary, we had to meet to prepare and sign the next invitation and to devise the programme for the forth-coming meeting. When the president came to see me, I offered him home-made *Vanilien Kipferl* (vanilla crescents) and slivovitz, in compliance with the well-tried axiom of reaching a man's heart through his stomach. The president was Franz Levi, who has now been my husband for the past 24 years. We are indeed lucky to be so well-matched and we are a truly happy couple.

That solved the question of studying for a degree. In gratitude, Franz and I ran the club for the next three years and made a number of good friends. We arranged for speakers on all sorts of subjects, discussions, and coffee-evenings. It was most enjoyable and, as far as I know, there was one other couple who came together after meeting at the club. But the problem of too many women and not enough men proved to be the club's eventual undoing. It was good while it lasted.

13 • *Death of a son*

Ilan and Franz met in Israel and took to each other immediately. I had gone to Israel for a refresher course in Hebrew soon after I had met Franz. When the course was over, Franz joined me and we had three weeks together in which we decided that I should obtain a divorce and that as soon as I was free, we would marry. This was in September 1969. We set up house together immediately after our return to London and were married on 3 October 1970.

When we were first in Israel, Ilan was in Greece. For some reason he left in a hurry and came to Israel to see me. He also decided to refresh his knowledge of Hebrew and enrolled at a very exposed border *kibbutz-ulpan*. Before he left for the course, we had three days together in Eilat, where Ilan and Franz got to know and respect each other. Ilan thought that I should have left Stephan a long time ago, and he was very pleased about my future plans with Franz.

After a few weeks in Israel, Ilan returned home to London and took a temporary job at the Medical Research Council, before going up to Oxford. He still had difficulties with girls. At the MRC, he met a young woman a few years older than himself with whom he began an affair. Ilan's friends, male or female, were always welcome in our home. Teresa was a nice person, but after three weeks or so, Ilan told us he wanted to end the relationship because he was not in love and did not feel that they really had much in common. He was 21 years old at the time, and Teresa was 26. A few days later he went to Oxford to read for his doctorate. Shortly afterwards the young woman informed him that she was pregnant. Ilan was shattered; as far as he was concerned their affair was over and he certainly did not want to marry Teresa. He was strongly of the opinion that having a child should be planned and not just happen. He also argued that unless one's religious beliefs were strong, an accidental pregnancy should be terminated. He was ambitious, still very young, and busy building up a life and career for himself. He was certainly not ready to take on the responsibility of a wife and a child.

Ilan went to see Teresa's father to explain how he felt and why he could not marry his daughter. On the other hand, Teresa had decided to keep the child and I was asked if I wanted the responsibility of being a grandmother. I straightaway accepted the commitment with pleasure, with the understanding that I would not try to persuade Ilan into marriage. I had myself been unhappily married long enough to know such an arrangement should not be contracted. Nevertheless, I was very sad when the boy was born and Ilan refused to see him or have anything to do with him. Teresa was very brave and never asked Ilan for maintenance; her parents helped and, when we were permitted, so did we a little. We had developed a good relationship with Teresa.

But, alas, it was the end of my warm relationship with Ilan. Even though he had asked me whether I would countenance being a grandmother, he seemed unable to come to terms with the birth of his son. He loved children and felt bitter about having a son when he was not really ready for parenthood. At the beginning, he occasionally inquired about the child, but later adopted a hostile attitude and refused to speak of him. However, we saw Jonathan about four times a year and watched him grow into a beautiful child. When he was just over eight years old, his mother married and her husband adopted the boy. Our relationship with Teresa continued on a cordial basis. She brought her fiancé to meet us and solicited our approval of him, which we gladly accorded. I greatly appreciated this gesture. When they got married I wrote a letter to Teresa offering to renounce seeing Jonathan if she felt that it would be best for him, now that he was part of a new family. I said that, quite naturally, I would be sad not to see my grandson, if such were to be her decision. Teresa insisted that I should continue to see the boy as the child was fond of me and we had been on such good terms. Unfortunately, periodically, there were some hitches and I had no regular access to the boy, but these difficulties were sorted out. I am very fond of Jonathan who reminds me in every way of his father: he is just as bright and lovely as Ilan was at his age.

158

In the meantime, Ilan obtained his Oxford DPhil degree, and proceeded to California for post-doctoral study. On holiday in Mexico, he met a lovely French girl, Isabelle, and they fell in love. Shortly afterwards, Ilan transferred to the Pasteur Institute in Paris to enable him to be near Isabelle, who was on the point of finishing her studies. He had previously applied for a position at the University of Zurich and was appointed to a professorship there. Since Isabelle had just completed her studies in town planning and very much wanted to find employment, they had to marry, otherwise she would not have been able to obtain permission to work in Switzerland. Ilan would have preferred to delay the marriage. He was anxious to make his mark in his field of research, and that would have allowed him little time to devote to Isabelle. He wanted her to see him in his normal working environment. In the Pasteur Institute, through lack of space, he had been unable to pursue his experimental work and could only write research papers. This allowed him more time with Isabelle.

In 1977, in Zurich, she and Ilan had a daughter. Ilan adored Marina and was a devoted father. He often took her to the university and even tried to knit something for her. But Isabelle was very unhappy in Zurich and a year and half after Marina's birth she returned to Paris with the child. Ilan was devastated – torn between his work and his family. He had attained distinction in his research but a paper he delivered at this time was not well received. Although this is no uncommon occurrence for a researcher, he took the rebuff too much to heart. A superb new laboratory was being built for his use and he had been extremely successful in securing money for research. He seemed to have had a special aptitude for obtaining research funds. His work was genetic research on the muscles of the fruitfly (drosophila), and he developed new theories which were controversial, though some of his ideas were years later accepted by geneticists.

He produced a stream of research papers for publication and assumed greater responsibilities than he could handle. He had taken up his Zurich post at the age of 26 and was again a father at 28. Now, he was just 30; he worked in his laboratory for more than 18 hours a day, hardly leaving enough time for sleep. Before Isabelle returned to Paris, he had some carefree hours at weekends and a respite from unremitting work. Now, on Friday nights, he took the train to Paris and worked throughout the entire night for he could not sleep on trains. In Paris he had a busy time with his family, driving out into the country, often negotiating long traffic jams which were anything but relaxing. Then on Sunday night it was back to Zurich on the train. The pressure became too great.

In August 1978 Ilan attended an international conference on genetics in Moscow. As he had strong socialist sympathies he was very much looking forward to going to the USSR. During his stay his views changed drastically. The main reason was a letter, written in English, from the son of Sergei Kovalyov, a dissident biologist who had been sentenced in 1976 to seven years' hard labour, asking the members of the conference to show solidarity with his father and to voice their protest. The French group to which Ilan had attached himself (the English biologists were not represented and he was the only Swiss representative) decided to take up Kovalyov's cause. As the language of the conference was English, Ilan was asked to read the protest letter. He approached the American president of the conference to get permission to read it aloud, but was refused. At the end of the session Ilan sprang on to the rostrum, took hold of the microphone and announced that he intended nevertheless to read the letter and referred the conference to the Helsinki agreement on human rights. He expressed the hope that it would be translated into Russian and proceeded to read it in English. There was an uproar from the Soviet organisers. The microphone was switched off and Ilan was pulled off the rostrum. As this was the last session, the international press were present, and leading newspapers like *Le Monde* in France and *Le Soir* in Belgium highlighted the story. When he arrived in London, reporters from *The Times* and the *Daily Telegraph* were waiting to interview him and gave coverage to the incident. I was proud to share the admiration of many of the delegates for the courage he had shown.

While I was still married to Stephan, I had the impression that my husband had never quite grown up. My relationship with him was more that of a mother to a grown-up child than that of a wife. Stephan was a compulsive punster, a practice that irritated me almost beyond endurance. I did my best to keep my ears tightly shut to his palaver but failed more often than not. In the months leading up to our divorce, he had learned to do things for himself; I weaned him slowly, very slowly, knowing that one day he would have to manage on his own. During our entire marriage there was one thing with which I could never cope. If Stephan wanted attention and could not get it normally, he would resort to stratagems which I found unbearable. He would lie to me on any subject and make sure that I found out. And I always fell into the trap. He drove me almost crazy. I became rude and ill-natured, deteriorating into a person I utterly despised. I began to hate him for what he caused me to become. I had to get away from him.

When I approached Stephan for a divorce, he seemed to take it calmly. He only wanted to keep the cat and I naturally acceded to his wish. It was not very flattering to be traded for a cat after 23 years' service – for that is what I felt our marriage had been – but I was free. Once I was away from Stephan, we could remain friends, and whenever he needed advice or help he could call on me. On this basis, our relationship has endured ever since.

A few years later, the cat, having attained the magnificent age of 19, died, and Stephan broke down. His attachment to the animal seemed to have kept him sane. He also had some set-backs with the orchestra, but the cat's death was the last straw. He was on a visit to our home and we had our grandson with us when he completely broke down, weeping and grovelling so that we had to call a doctor to get him to hospital. After that, for several years, it was a series of ups and downs for him; when, eventually, the orchestra became unable to cope with his eccentricities he was retired.

In 1979, Stephan travelled with the orchestra to Lausanne for some concerts. Ilan decided to go to see him – it seemed important to him at that point to try to establish some human relationship with his father. Although greatly fatigued and reluctant to tear himself away from his punishing schedule, he nevertheless went to Lausanne to meet his father. I warned him on the phone that Stephan was in a very bad mental state, but Ilan insisted on seeing him. The meeting was catastrophic – Stephan proved to be unapproachable.

Ilan returned to Zurich a very disappointed man. It was the first time that he had spoken to anyone about his father – the relationship, or lack of it, must have been weighing heavily on him. At this time, Ilan was suffering from headaches and depression, and I tried to persuade him to seek medical help but he steadfastly refused. I offered to come and see him, but, as he intended to visit us in England, stopping at Paris on the way to bring Marina, his daughter, with him, he did not think there was any point in my going to Zurich. I had a telephone conversation with him on 25 July as to where and when I could meet them on their arrival in London. He told me that he had the tickets for the journey in his pocket. During the phone call he suddenly asked about his son – was he happy, was he well? I told him that Teresa had married and that Jonathan had been adopted. He replied that he hoped the boy would be happy. He was glad he had never met the lad, for he would not have been able to bear to be separated from both his children.

Four days after this conversation, on 29 July 1979, I was working in the garden when Franz called me. There was a telephone call: Ilan had had an accident and was dead. As it turned out, it was not an accident; he had taken an overdose of a poison which he used in his laboratory.

Time does not heal, though it does help to assuage one's loss, making it easier to bear. But it hurts; the waste of it all – the senselessness. I sometimes get so angry with Ilan even today, but mostly I pity him for what he had to endure, and I feel sad that I was not permitted at least to try to help him.

A few of Ilan's papers were published posthumously. An encyclopaedia on the drosophila which was due for publication had many references to him, so I am told. In 1989, when I was clearing out Stephan's flat (he was then in a mental hospital and was being transferred to an old people's home, where he is now well settled and looked after), a letter arrived for Stephan from Oxford. When I read it to him, we were deeply moved. It was from Professor Henry Harris, with whom Ilan had studied for his doctorate in 1972. Professor Harris wanted us to know that a research group in Japan had used Ilan's work as the basis of their study on the nucleolus (a minute rounded body within the nucleus of a cell in animal or vegetable substance). In their manuscript they referred to Ilan's paper of 1972, acknowledging it as the forerunner in their current experiments. How thoughtful of Professor Harris to tell us about this! Ten years after Ilan's death, his work was still of importance! It was heartbreaking to think that one so gifted had lived for a brief 30 years.

His two children, who to my great regret did not get to know each other until 1991 (when Jonathan was 20 and Marina 14), remain to remind me of what a remarkable person Ilan was. I blame Hitler for his death. Because of the Holocaust Ilan lacked the support which grandparents and an extended family normally provide. Even from me he was constantly separated through all the predicaments. I am convinced that if I had been able to give him more security and a feeling of belonging, he would not have been driven to an early death.

Fortunately, I have Franz, who gives me a reason to carry on. And after nearly 50 years of bouts of fear and terror at night, I am now even able – on most nights – to sleep without tranquillisers or sleeping pills.

Life goes on, and I enjoy much of it on the surface. That, I suppose, is more than many people can say. My inner life, that of the concentration camp, living with a schizophrenic and as the mother of a dead son, rarely shows itself to the outside world. That should be enough.

Epilogue

I had started working with the Overseas Development Institute in 1965. It was the only time that I worked in a non-Jewish intellectual environment and it was most refreshing. The staff were intelligent, kind and friendly and very civilised. It was a time when the African colonies were in the process of becoming independent. It was an exciting time seeing the changes and hopes of these newly emerging countries in a most sympathetic atmosphere. During my first stint of about ten months I worked as assistant to the librarian. In my second stint of only about two and a half months I worked on indexing some publications and helping one of the researchers. I learned a lot during my time there.

I was lured away to work for the Leo Baeck Institute by the brilliant and charming Dr Robert Weltsch who at the time needed some help with the publication of the Leo Baeck Year Book. The Leo Baeck Institute was at the time, and I suppose still is, researching mainly into the German Jewish symbiosis. For eight months I was reading and correcting articles, then proofs and finally preparing the index for a couple of volumes of the year book. When that work ended Dr Weltsch asked me to take notes for his correspondence. This was rather unfortunate for I had told him right at the beginning that I was unable to take shorthand. So we parted company and I returned to the Overseas Development Institute for my second stint. However, I saw that there was not much future for the existence of ODI as an important research institute and that they would probably have to reduce staff. ODI had been of great importance while the Conservatives were in power. When Labour was voted in they created a Ministry of Overseas Development and ODI became a rather peripheral institute.

I registered my name with an agency for university graduates. I told them that my university education was never completed but I had quite a bit of knowledge in various fields and had a number of languages. They accepted me on to their books, and kept notifying me of various jobs. I applied for most of them but mostly did not even get an interview. Until one day they sent me a note about an archive job at the Library of University College, London.

After so many disappointments I thought I would have no chance and I did not even apply. Then, about ten days later, I decided that I really had nothing to lose and wrote a one-page letter including a short CV. I did not even bother to reread it, though naturally I wrote only about my true experiences. Next day I had a telephone call from the Librarian's secretary: when would it be convenient for me to come to see the Librarian? I was puzzled. I went to see Mr Scott, the Librarian, who was most charming. He thought – so he said – that I was exactly what he was looking for. When could I start and how much time could I give – the job was part-time. We agreed on my starting to work on the Gaster papers.

Dr Gaster, who came originally from Romania, had been the Haham, or Chief Rabbi, of the Spanish and Portuguese Jews in Great Britain. Besides this he was a polyhistor. He lived from 1856 to 1939, and from 1885 in England. He was in correspondence with personalities from all over the world and in many languages. Much of his correspondence was in Romanian. Dr Gaster had never thrown away any papers that came into his house, and now this correspondence was deposited at UCL, waiting to be organised into an archive. I still have a slight suspicion that I was accepted for the job because someone had mixed up Budapest with Bucharest. Perhaps it was assumed that I would automatically know Romanian, Hungary – where I came from – being next to Romania.

The material was kept in the Mocatta Library. This was a beautiful, old, purpose-built library established and built by the Jewish Historical Society of England. The Mocatta Library has since been relocated into another part of the main library, together with the other Jewish material at UCL, thus forming the Jewish Studies Library. I was at first rather sad about this arrangement because it was in the original library that I spent the next 22 years working on the Gaster Papers comprising some 170,000 items, as well as becoming involved with the work of the library itself. Eventually I was put in charge of the Mocatta Library, as well as of the Jewish and Hebrew collections at University College, London's main library. I very much enjoyed the work both with the archive and with the libraries until my retirement in 1988.

At the same time I did some freelance work such as the two bibliographies for the Survey of Jewish Affairs, published by the World Jewish Congress, as well as some work for the Central Zionist Archives, and the Weizmann Letters. I am occasionally invited to speak to various bodies – children, university students, societies, historical and charitable, teachers, or an odd conference. The themes I speak about are the Jewish material at University College, London, the genealogical material which was at the Mocatta Library, and the Holocaust. I never thought that I would be capable of speaking in front of a group of people, and even less that I would be capable of answering questions at these occasions. Yet, I seem to be quite successful in expressing myself, because there are always more questions asked after my talks than time permits, which shows that I have aroused the interest of my listeners. This gives me great pleasure.

Since my retirement I started to learn to play the piano – something I always wanted to do. I am also a volunteer to visit lonely old persons and to help where I can. From the beginning of 1993 I began attending a course in creative writing, mainly producing short stories, which seem to give some pleasure to those to whom I read them. The result of one of the exercises is the following poem:

OBITUARY

Her motto was: do not worry about what has passed
about events one cannot change.
Life's ups and downs she took in her stride;
When decisions had to be made
she did not take them lightly
and took the consequences.
She tried to help when it was feasible
She lived every day with its joys and worries
Never took anything for granted and therefore
got pleasure from the smallest of life's gifts.

Epilogue

Her tolerance got thinner as she got older
Though her patience remained throughout.
She had to have music,
beautiful things to look at
good conversation, good people,
nature's wonders, water and mountains,
flowers and fruits, trees and stones.
the warmth of the sun, looking for crystals,
mushrooms or berries. Also good food.
She enjoyed cooking: her friends had to suffer
for the flights of her imagination,
with herbs and spices she wasted her time
never worrying about their waist-line.
She wanted no grave, but to be cremated
dispersed and quietly disappear.
Dust to dust. No religious speeches, no prayers
Let her go in peace and if by any chance
there is incarnation which she did not believe in
to be a spoilt cat would have been her wish.
A cat with its independent nature, sleek
handsome and playful but not a hunter
that catches birds and mice,
just curled up in someone's lap, beloved.
She would even oblige by purring her thanks.

Trude Levi
21 October 1993

167

Notes

1. *Mephisto*, a film made from the novel by Klaus Mann. The figure of Hoefgen is based on the life of the German actor Gruendgens, who though originally a decent human being is slowly manipulated through fear and ambition into being a pawn in the Hitler regime.
2. Primo Levi, *If this is a man* (London: Abacus, 1987), p. 91.
3. A film by Charlie Chaplin, where Chaplin works with two pliers on a conveyor belt, and shows the reaction to the automatic work.
4. Dieter Vaupel, a German history teacher, who made a project with his pupils about what had happened during the Nazi era at Hessisch-Lichtenau. As a result of his research a memorial stone was erected near the camp-site in memory of the 1,000 Hungarian Jewesses, who were brought there from Auschwitz to work in the nearby munitions factory.
5. Dieter Vaupel, *Das Aussenkommando Hessisch Lichtenau des Konzentrationslagers Buchenwald 1944/45. Eine Dokumentation* (Kassel: Verlag Gesamthochschulbibliothek, 1984). Nationalsozialismus in Nordhessen. Schriften zur regionalen Zeitgeschichte, Heft 3.
6. Young Gentiles of military age were exempt from military service while completing their studies, but this did not apply to Jews. Thus these young men were able to complete their studies.
7. Nansen passport: a certificate of identification agreed on in Geneva on 5 July 1922, by Germany, Austria and Switzerland. Originally instituted for Russian refugees who became stateless. Called after Fridjof Nansen, who dealt with the problems of the refugees.
8. The *Freedom Charter* launched in 1955 by the non-racial South African Congress was considered treasonable by the South African regime. One hundred and fifty-six people were arrested and charged. The trial lasted from 1956 to 1961. Treason could not be proved and all the accused were eventually discharged.
9. *Kashrut*: food which has been prepared according to Jewish religious laws. Restrictions include the non-mixing of milk and meat substances and the consumption of certain animals, poultry and fish. The guidelines are to be found in the Old Testament Book of Leviticus, Chapter xi.